NONE SUCH LIKE IT

AN ENLIGHTENING VOYAGE THROUGH THE NINE STAGES OF BOAT-BUYING GRIEF

Annie Dike

None Such Like It

To the friend who forbids me to write good books.
"Don't be good. Be great."

Table of Contents

Prologue

It started with shock. Our buddy was so euphoric about the idea of owning his very own live-aboard sailboat, he envisioned himself aboard the only one in the world that simply could not sink. "Thru-hulls? Oh hush, nothing goes through my hull." I have to admit, when he first came to us with the idea, I was a little shocked myself. *Mr. While You're Down There with his very own boat?*

Anyone else I could understand, but this was Mitch, the man with such patterned and predictable requests for retrieval of provisions from below he had earned himself the "Down There" nickname. Mitch had squeezed and wiggled around our boat like a grown man in a McDonald's PlayPlace and often needed a bucket hanging from his neck to upchuck his Doritos. *This man wants a boat?* I'm not one to shoot a man's horse, but there are just some people you know—and they can be very close friends, hearts of gold, good, salt of the earth people—but you just *know*, they should not own a boat. It's just not a good fit.

Mitch can't sit still for five minutes. He cannot *not* ask questions any time you do anything. "What's that?" "Where does it go?" "Why are you *turning* it?" He's got the best of intentions but he's also got some sort of halo filter around his head that makes him perceive only his surroundings, only his emergencies. "Patience is a ..." you can start to say, but he'll cut you off before you finish with a "Hang on," a "Hold this," or "Move!"

I know all of this because Mitch was the third member of our rookie crew during the shakedown of all shakedowns, for us at least, in 2013 when Phillip and I sailed our recently-purchased 1985 Niagara 35 home from Punta Gorda, Florida to Pensacola across the Gulf of Mexico. Although I've been told "along the edge of" the Gulf is more accurate than "across," it doesn't have quite the adventurous ring to it! And I'm stubborn. So, consider them synonymous for purposes of this fine treatise. I also say "rookie crew" because there were so many things the three of us had not done, or had not done *together*, which would have better prepared us for that passage. I, for one, had never sailed. Aside from a one-hour romp on another boat Phillip and I had looked at before settling on the Niagara, that trip was the second sail of my entire life. That meant I had no sailing experience, no offshore experience, no experience to speak of at all. Everything was new to me. Sometimes I still wonder why Phillip let me come along. Maybe to clean and cook? I would have been okay with that.

While Mitch had some sailing experience, he had never been on an offshore passage and he and Phillip had never sailed together, nor had he sailed a boat like ours. While Phillip was easily the most experienced of the three of us in handling a large sailboat, he had never captained a boat on an offshore passage and had never been on a passage this long before. And, as Phillip repeatedly stressed: "Every boat is different." Meaning, no matter how much experience you may have, each time you step aboard a boat you've never sailed before, there is a learning curve. So, the three of us—Phillip, Mitch and I—were sailing a boat we had never sailed before, with a crew that had never sailed together before on a passage none of us had undertaken before. Nothing could go wrong, right? *Wrong.*

Plenty did and, while I'm not sure I would want it to all play out the same way again, it did make for one hell of a story. And, at the beating heart of it was him: Mr. "While You're Down There." He was easily the most colorful character on that trip, the loudest too. And while Phillip and I both will be forever grateful for his help in bringing our boat back home in mostly one piece, to be honest, the thought of Mitch with his own boat kind of frightened us. It's just such a huge commitment. It's a huge money pit. Plus, it's huge! The image of Mitch barreling up to our boat in some thirty-plus foot tank shouting and trying to raft up gave me nightmares. *"Hang on!" "Hold this!" "Move!"* Then I woke to the sound of crunching fiberglass.

But it did not matter how many times we tried to tell him we just didn't think it would be the right move for him. "Try a charter for the weekend," we told him. "Don't jump right into this," we warned. It did not work. Mitch set his sights on a boat down in Ft. Myers, put in an offer sight unseen, hit the road and just went ahead and bought a boat while he was down there. *Only Mitch.*

But Phillip and I knew we had a debt to pay. Mitch had stepped up when no one else had or could to help us bring our beautiful Niagara back from south Florida, so he knew we would step up and do the same for him when it came time to bring his own boat home across the Gulf.

I knew, at the very least, it would make for one hell of a story with the colorful and charismatic Mitch now playing the role of Captain. What I was not prepared for, however, was the enlightening journey Phillip and I would embark on during the process with Mitch through the nine stages of his boat-buying grief. First Mitch was in shock. Then he was angry. Other times he seemed to deny the whole thing ever happened, like he didn't just buy a magnificent never-ending chore that needed to be stocked, cleaned, maintained and repaired.

For the first time I started to see my-dumb-self experiencing each of those phases when Phillip and I had purchased and began cruising our own boat just two years prior and it dawned on me. I was Mitch once. You likely have been, too. Once you've made your own voyage through the stages, though, and accepted the fantastically-frustrating reality of boat ownership, friends who seek to follow you down this seemingly insane path provide endless entertainment when their boats—as boats tend to do—start giving them plenty of grief.

CHAPTER ONE

SHOCK

The Surreal Belief That Boats Mean Only Fun

The affected's initial reaction may be numbness or a surreal sensation, as if what just happened did not, in fact, happen at all. He may feel as though he is not entirely present or emotionally attached to what is happening.

We've all had it happen to a friend at one point or another. They see you have a boat. They come and hang out a time or two on your boat. They start asking you questions about maintenance, where you keep it, how much this costs, how much that costs. Then it happens. It's inevitable. Your friend gets bit. Now he wants a sailboat too.

Then he drives you crazy. It's all he can think about. All he can talk about. He drives his wife mad. He spends every free minute, even to the early hours of the morning, poring over listings on Craigslist,

Yachtworld, broker sites, even eBay—trolling his fair share of "boat porn." They should have a support group for the addicts. The hunt is consuming.

Now usually such a friend doesn't actually take the plunge. It's easy for him to shop, compare, research, ask a hundred questions but when it comes time to actually choose a boat and put in an offer, most of these "bitten" friends find the urge is not quite strong enough. They talk a big game, but when it comes time to actually sign up with a broker and put in an offer, the urge wanes. But, while they are "seriously shopping"—so they claim—and while you don't think this particular friend should really own a boat—so you claim—it's too tempting to not encourage them. *Imagine the entertainment*, your mind teases. You can't help it. Do you allow your devilish intrigue to take over?

"Of course you should get one, Jim. Sailboats are awesome. They're fun 100% of the time and they never give you problems," you say through a slick smile.

Now why do you say that? Because you've been there! You've been Jim, that googley-eyed boat-struck sucker who wouldn't listen to or heed any warnings. *I'm getting a boat darnit!* And because you were that person and you got a boat (darnit!) and then realized, like everyone told you, that it was one of the most expensive, frustrating, fantastic things you've ever done, you can now kick back and settle into your new role as Jim's friend—the tried, tested and proven boat owner—and get a little entertainment out of Jim's voyage down the same path. Even though you know he won't listen, you may try to wise your poor friend to the realities of boat ownership.

"Now, it's a lot of hard work, Jim. It's going to be very costly, especially in the beginning but it will continue to always cost you more than you expected. It also requires a lot of time and labor. It needs to be your biggest time and money commitment. Are you sure you're ready for that?"

You might do the latter because you're a good person and you really care about poor Jim and his continued financial, mental and marital stability. Or you might do it because you know if he *does* get a boat and it *does* in fact give him problems—s*hocker!*—the first person he's going to bring those problems to is you.

But you've got your own boat, remember? Your own daily host of boat problems. You don't need his too. Sometimes, though, no matter how hard you try to talk Jim out of it—ease him back from that ledge—he is inclined to take the plunge anyway. No matter how much you "say" it's going to cost him (he says with fake quotation marks and a snarl, mocking you), he thinks he's ready. He's getting a boat darnit! If that's the case, you might as well jump on the bandwagon and help him. You know, at the very least, it's going to be one hell of a show.

That's where Phillip and I were. After the three of us, Phillip, Mitch and I, made the initial epic Gulf-crossing bringing our Niagara 35 from Punta Gorda, Florida to her home port in Pensacola, Mitch really did swear he would never get back on our boat with us again to cross anything. "Anything." Those were his words. And he didn't. Never again for a passage. But, he did get on our boat again a time or two when we invited him and his family out for the occasional weekend to enjoy the brighter side of cruising—life on the hook, hourly dives off

the bow into crystal-green warm waters, grilling burgers in the cockpit, eating dinner under a smattering of stars, falling asleep to the sound of the wind and water lapping at your hull. He kicked back on our deck— all Havana daydreaming—and that's when it happened. It really was inevitable.

Mitch got bit. He wanted a sailboat too.

Oh boy. At first, Phillip and I kind of scoffed at the idea and laughed it off. While Mitch is a good sailor, he is still—we knew from firsthand experience—a screamer, a slapper and certainly a *big* person to fit on a little boat. Scratch that. Any boat. I had to wonder, though, if folks thought the same of me when Phillip and I were boat shopping and I couldn't tell you the bow from the stern, the main sail from the jib, the ... anything from the anything else. I called lines "ropes" for Christ's sake! When we found our beautiful Niagara down in Punta Gorda, Florida, the first thing I asked, all doe-eyed and innocent, was "When will they deliver the boat to us, Phillip?" I'm sure at that stage, *I* was the person my boating friends believed "should never own a boat."

To be honest, we simply didn't think Mitch's desire for a live-aboard sailboat would really come to fruition. At the time, he owned a little Sea Pearl 21. It was one of those "saw it for sale on the side of the road" type deals he'd picked up for a steal and it seemed to just be an experiment to see whether the family would like sailing—one I believe ended badly. The Pearl was very small, a trailer-able, open day-sailer, and quite a rocky, rolly boat for him and his family. I have yet to tip a sailboat but this was the first one I really thought I might.

He took Phillip and me out in the Sea Pearl one sunny afternoon in Pensacola Bay right after he bought it and, as I suspected, there was plenty of "Hang on!" "Hold this!" and "Move!" Mitch was like an unpredictable rogue ballast. Anytime he moved from one side of the boat to the other—which he did often for no reason other than he's fidgety—the boat threatened to tip. If you didn't somehow lunge your body weight immediately to the other side of the boat, she would swamp on Mitch's side. And I say "lunge your body weight" because it was not a dainty procession. These were not the ginger steppings of a girl at her cotillion. This was more like a mosh pit. If Mitch made the slightest indication of a move, Phillip or I would throw our torso toward the opposite rail and just lay for a minute until Mitch settled back in.

"Now won't this be perfect for the family?" Mitch asked, a goofy grin pointed up toward the sails completely unaware of the lunge-and-leap act Phillip and I had been putting on. Phillip and I were splayed out

on the starboard side trying to hide our faces from him.

Yeah Mitch. Just perfect.

We weren't there for the inaugural test trial with the family aboard the Sea Pearl, but Mitch said when he took his wife, Michelle, out on the Pearl she looked about as comfortable "as a cat in the bathtub." His words. Apparently, when the family—not quite as trained on the "wherever Mitch goes, go the opposite" rule—darn near tipped the little skiff over, it was so traumatic for Michelle that she vowed to never set foot on a boat with Mitch again. *"But what about this?"* I could just hear him saying to Michelle in the face of her refusal. Ever the negotiator, he was somehow able to massage her ultimatum into an arrangement wherein she was never required to step aboard *that* boat again, the Sea Pearl. In return, Mitch got an agreement that she would step aboard a boat with him again, so long as it was "un-tippable." Her words. With that settled, there really was nothing else Mitch could do but embark on a hunt for a bigger, un-tippable boat.

I think once he officially decided this is what he was going to do—buy a boat—that's when Mitch entered stage one: shock. While Phillip and I agreed the Pearl was definitely the wrong boat for the 6'4" Roberts and his family, we were not yet convinced any boat would be, but Mitch had succumbed to the delirium. He sold the cute little rocky-rolly boat and did what those bitten do: started scouring listings, shopping online until midnight, looking at boats in marinas around town. It was all he could think about. All he could talk about. Phillip and I tried, initially, to talk him back from the ledge. "It's a lot of work buddy. A *lot* of work."

I kept conjuring images of Mitch trying to execute what to him might be an impossible boat project. I saw him sticking—arms and legs—out of a lazarette, fumbling for a wayward screw in the bilge, rubber-glove clad, dry-heaving at the sight of the treasures that awaited him in the holding tank and it brought me back to my own ignorant euphoria and the many times Phillip had tried to convey that to *me* when we were—like Mitch—just toying with the idea of really buying a boat.

"Owning a boat is a lifestyle," Phillip would say. "If you really want to maximize it, it has to be the primary way you want to spend your money, your time, your … money." And while he was right, I didn't truly "get it" when he said these things to me. I was focused on the more important task of choosing the captain's hat that looked best on me. Did I picture myself holed up in the engine room fighting a greasy steering cable? No. Could I envision myself trying to wiggle ass-first into a lazarette? Heck no! I didn't even know what a lazarette was at the time. Now, were all of the projects and work and effort Phillip tried to warn me about worse than I had imagined? Somewhat. But were they impossible? No. And they certainly snapped me out of my blissful *'This hat or that?''* stage. I hoped this would turn out to be the same for Mitch because he was clearly in the same surreal state of mind.

Every time he talked about getting a boat we would warn him again about how much it would cost, how much time it would take to maintain it, how hard it would be, how much it would cost. (Yes, again.) But none of it stuck. Mitch waved us off time and again. Our words seemed to strike him like little pebbles and clatter uselessly to the floor. No matter how graphic or realistic our warnings ("You may have to physically un-clog the head," "You may have to dole out three grand in a day") he had no emotional reaction to them. He was living in a surreal world where boats meant only fun.

No matter what we said Mitch persisted, until finally his persistence won us over. It became clear Mitch was going—hell or high water—to get himself a boat. It was kind of inspiring actually. Even in the face of stern advice, it was like Mitch knew he wanted this. It seemed he needed it. We couldn't stop him. So we joined him.

"We might as well help him get a good one," Phillip finally conceded, "because you know we're going to be the first ones he'll call when stuff starts to break." And that was it. Phillip and I were officially enlisted as Mitch's trusted boat counsel.

Mitch's number-one requirement—as it is with most folks in the market—was something affordable. That's usually first and foremost. But his next item of importance was a boat he could single-hand. While his significant other is a sprite, attractive lady, a sailor she was not nor did she express any desire to be, which is fine. It's not for everyone. And, at ten years old, Mitch's son—while he may someday become a great sailor—didn't yet have the knowledge or strength to truly help Mitch handle a boat. Initially, it would be Mitch manning the entire vessel himself, so his primary concern was a boat that was large enough to fit them all comfortably, including his sizeable self, but that he could also handle and sail by himself.

He also wanted a boat that was essentially "turn-key." "Just toss the lines and she's ready to go," he would say, which gave me a chuckle. Granted there are many boats out there like that, but "Go for how much?" I wanted to ask him to remind him of his own stern, line-in-the-sand budget. And, "Go for how long?" Before you have to dole out some bucks for repairs. Usually when you first buy a boat, there is a list of initial upgrades, improvements or repairs that you want to undertake right out of the gate to really make the boat your own. If there are not (which is rare), there is still the usual maintenance and upkeep ticker that is always going and it would be hard to fathom any one of those small or not-so-small projects hadn't reached its prime while the boat sat for sale.

"Oh stop it Negative Nancy," Mitch would say with a whiff of his hand when I tried to tell him these things. "*Uhh ... no. Try Realistic Rita,*" I wanted to counter but I would just hold my hands up in the air and shake my head. *What more could I do?* While I understood Mitch did not have the time, knowledge or money to dump into a fixer-upper and I would not want that for him—mostly because I would not want that (Mitch with a monster project) for *us*, I was not sure he would be able to find a boat that would be ready to go, maintenance free, for an entire season, within his price range. I won't disclose the specifics. Just know Mitch is a savvy negotiator and can strike some killer deals. I think it's his wily charm that wins folks over. And, he had a vision for the type of boat he was confident he would be able to find within his very tight price range. I just found it a tall order was all, but perhaps my Nancy was showing because the man was also lucky. Irritatingly lucky.

With the single-handed sailing requirement, one of the first boats Mitch considered was a Nonsuch. It's a cat rig boat with a very simple set-up. Think one big sail. Seriously, that's it. Once you hoist the sail, there is nothing more to do than trim it. How do you tack? You turn the wheel. That's all. The boat handles the rest. Phillip and I were kind of intrigued by the idea. *Just one sail? That must make it easy, right?* We'll get back to that.

It was, however, a Hinterhoeller—the same make as our boat—so of course Phillip and I gave Mitch a thumbs-up there. And, it was Hinterhoeller's flagship model. Compared to the number of Nonsuches they produced, the Niagaras were a mere fraction. There's something to take away from that. If they weren't well-received by the sailing public, they wouldn't keep making them, right? But, it's not a very common boat. At least not around the Florida panhandle. I had never seen one before. I would recall if I did. It looks awfully funny—with that big tree-trunk mast at the very front of the boat and no stays. Not a one.

The huge, hulky mast stands of its own accord, like a pine in the wind. And I had no idea initially that "wishbone" thingy could even qualify as a "boom."

We had yet to see a Nonsuch sailing around in Pensacola. I was sure of that. You couldn't miss it or forget it if you did. The first sight of it, from the pictures Mitch sent, made me do a double take. But, often so does Mitch, so I guess it was fitting.

But because they were rare in our parts, Mitch struggled to find a Nonsuch close to home to set foot on. Most of the ones he did find that were even worth a look were hundreds of miles away. For this reason, Mitch finally conceded to at least set foot on some other types of boats that were available for sale in our local marinas so he could start to get a feel for what might work for him. Granted, he did not yet have a physical "feel" for the Nonsuch, but he had an intuition.

In all of his boat-buying process, Mitch stepped aboard exactly one other boat: a late-eighties Hunter 34 located in Pensacola. It was a boat for sale in our marina, actually, so Mitch set up a look-see (real technical term in sailing—you look at the boat and see what you find). Curious about Mitch's intentions and probably wanting the entertainment of experiencing boat-shopping through Mitch's eyes, Phillip signed up for the look-see and what he and Mitch found was Mitch didn't fit. The Hunter was a good boat, in good condition for its age, but Mitch literally hung head-and-shoulders off of the vberth bed. While this alone was a telltale sign, Mitch said overall the boat just didn't feel right for him.

It is definitely a very subjective thing, whether you step on a boat and it "feels right" to you. I remember when Phillip and I stepped aboard our Niagara. I was so new to boats in general at that time, I wasn't even sure I knew what I, personally, was looking for. Phillip mentioned the cockpit offered "good bracing for heeling" and, I swear, one of the first things that came to mind was a band of Baptist revivalists wedging themselves against the backrests while dousing someone in the cockpit floor with holy water. I tried to hide moments like that with a blank stare, but it soon kicked in. *Oh, heeling. As in "leaning over." Got it.* Even at that state of boat ignorance, though, I could tell the Niagara felt comfortable, warm, right.

Phillip and I were curious, though, what 'feeling' Mitch was really aiming for. Build quality? Comfort? Seaworthiness? Decor? We had no way to know. And, for someone new to live-aboard boats, it's often hard to know what characteristics of a boat will be important to you or what ones you thought would be important turn out to be irrelevant. I've met people boat-shopping who say the number one factor they want in a boat is air conditioning. You might laugh because that characteristic is not even exclusive to a boat. *If you want AC, go buy a condo!* you scoff. But, what about comfort? That is definitely something you want in a boat. And that characteristic is not boat-specific either. Having met many people in the market for a boat, I have found whatever people *believe* they want in a boat will drive their search, whether it turns out to be something that is important to them later or not. You can't really talk them out of what they think they will like, even if it is three heads and two AC units.

That was definitely the case with Mitch. For whatever reason, all roads kept leading him back to the Nonsuch. He had a firm belief it would be the right boat for him. Phillip and I knew very little about the Nonsuch but, seeing as how it was a Hinterhoeller we didn't give it the Negative Nancy 'no.' We knew, at the very least, the it would be good build quality and a dependable boat for our insatiable new sailboat buddy.

I guess if you call boat-shopping online looking at "boat porn," it seemed Mitch had developed a rare, un-treatable Nonsuch fetish. He searched high and low and finally found one down in Ft. Myers, Florida—suitable driving range from Pensacola—that had been on the market for quite some time. It was a 1985, like ours as well (*I know, kind of eerie*), but it appeared to be in good condition. The man who owned it sailed it often. Reportedly all systems worked. No big repairs, overhauls or major modifications were needed. The selling broker told Mitch the boat was just as it appeared in the photos which—minus a little elbow grease and Simply Green—was astonishingly good.

The selling broker also told Mitch the owner was motivated. *That's where he went wrong.* While Mitch is quite the character—entertaining, comical at times, loud and impulsive—he is also a born salesman. He's so enigmatic, such a dominating vibrant personality, you can't really work your way around him. After a while, you just give in. I wouldn't even use those tired ice-to-Eskimos or ketchup-to-a-white-gloved-lady lines. No. Mitch could sell you the sweaty, oversized tank top off his back and soon have you his selling the rest of his soppy shirts on commission. He's that good.

With the word 'motivated,' Mitch was motivated. He put in an offer for half the asking price. Yes, *half.* I was annoyed at the thought of it. I won't even tell you the asking price so you won't have to be annoyed by it either. I mentioned the irritatingly-lucky part. But, it made Phillip and me a little skeptical. Why would such a good boat (according to the pictures) in such great condition (according to the broker) go for such a great price? It sounded a little too good to be true.

Not to Mitch, though. I was surprised he wasn't more worried or scared. He seemed numb to the fact that he had just legally obligated himself to buy a boat that might be half-sunk. I couldn't *not* imagine Mitch walking up to this too-good-to-be-true Nonsuch and finding it half full of water, that big sail only a shredded, tattered remain and the water line sitting right below the toe rail on the outside. I could hear the gurgle as he walked up. Apparently that's not the sight Mitch had in his mind, though, because he did it. An old Nonsuch sitting down in Ft. Myers, and Mitch "While You're Down There" Roberts—in a state of blissfully-ignorant shock—puts in an offer. Sight unseen.

CHAPTER TWO

DENIAL

The Impractical Conviction That Your Boat Cannot Sink

Once the shock diminishes, the affected may feel frantic with the gravity of what has just occurred. He may refuse to believe anything has happened, deny the truth and pretend nothing has changed.

"Did he inspect all of the thru-hulls?"

"Yes."

"Did he run the bilge pump?"

"Yes."

"Did you guys try to reef the sail?"

"Well ..."

Mitch was down in Ft. Myers, reporting back to us after the survey/ sea-trial of the Nonsuch. Phillip was running Mitch through the paces after the trial and he was passing with flying colors *until* he got to the reefing. We'll get back to that.

Not one week after Mitch put in his low-ball, sight-unseen offer, he made the ten-hour trek from Pensacola down to Ft. Myers to have his first look at the Nonsuch and attend the survey sea/trial and it turned out the selling broker had been right. The seller *was* motivated. Even at half the asking price—albeit contingent on a satisfactory survey/sea trial—the owner accepted. Now it was Phillip and I who were shocked. Surely Mitch's luck would run soon.

We didn't want to think it, but even if she *looked* great, I had the image of the whole transom blowing off when they turned the engine over for the first time—I presumed—in several years. I envisioned Mitch trying to raise a sail that looked like a slice of Swiss cheese. I heard the cracking sound as the rudder snapped off the first time he turned into the wind. I couldn't stop my mind from conjuring these sights and sounds. Then I heard Mitch's very voice creep in and scold me: *"Shut up Negative Nancy!"*

We could tell from Mitch's actual voice that he was truly excited about the Nonsuch. It seemed the survey/sea-trial had been a small-time adventure for him. He was mesmerized by the boat, its condition, its performance, even its owner.

"Now this guy. He's like eighty. Maybe eighty-two," Mitch said, which cracked me up. *How is eighty so different from eighty-two?* "And he's hopping up and down all over the boat faster than I can, completely un-winded, like a monkey off his leash. Then, *then!*" Mitch nearly shouts. "He apologizes for being a little late because he had a tennis match that morning."

You could hear the bewilderment in Mitch's voice. *An eighty year-old who plays tennis. I'm sorry, eighty-two. Who knew?* I was going to get a kick out of seeing Mitch meet so many of the cruisers Phillip and I have met, well into their seventies, who can work circles around us. Cruising will do that to you. Apparently, owning, maintaining and single-handing a thirty-foot Nonsuch will do that to you as well. For some reason though, I just couldn't get myself to picture Mitch all sprite and tennis player-like hopping around on deck. This was the man I described as Neal Armstrong landing on the moon when he stepped around overhead on the decks of our Niagara. I was hoping at the very least, though, that the sight of this sinewy, leathered Nonsuch owner would force Mitch to recall the many times we had told him "It's going to be a lot of work buddy. A lot of work."

"I need to pick up tennis," was all he said.

The only real issue the surveyor noted was some rotting of the rub rail on the starboard side and an area where the strut that holds the propeller shaft attaches to the hull that would need some fiberglass repair, but there was no water intrusion. Otherwise, the boat's integrity was solid. She fired right up for the sea-trial, Mitch said the boat sailed very well and the surveyor gave the 1985-year-old gal a clean bill of health.

It almost worried me it was starting to come to fruition: Mr. While You're Down There with his very own sailboat. I still found the thought wildly radical, but Phillip and I knew, if everything went well with the survey/sea trial, that Mitch was going to buy that boat. And Mitch probably knew Phillip and I—being the salty fiends we are—would help him bring his boat back home safely across the Gulf which likely played a big part in his willingness to buy a boat nearly four hundred nautical miles away.

Having gone through the process of trying to outfit a new-to-us boat for a pretty extensive offshore passage with the Niagara, Phillip and I knew, if we were going to be making this trip with Mitch, that that we needed to start making lists early. It's amazing the things you remember to bring the *second* time around. Before Mitch even went down to Ft. Myers, Phillip and I jotted down critical safety equipment, spare parts and other items that would be needed for the boat and crew to safely make the passage from Ft. Myers to Pensacola so Mitch could verify whether any of the items were already on the boat while he was there for the survey/sea trial. We sent Mitch with our rudimentary checklist and told him to inventory the items, note what was missing and what might need to be replaced, replenished or re-certified before we headed offshore in the Nonsuch.

While Mitch really was taking it all like a champ, checking and double-checking the list with us, I knew he was having trouble understanding the real need for some of these things.

"Nerf balls," Mitch screeched at me over the phone one day while he was getting ready to make the trip down to Ft. Myers, and I figured that was a reasonable question if he didn't know that that magically-squishy material, an accidental invention by NASA I'm sure, is wickedly effective at stopping leaks. But, *figuring* when it comes to Mitch is where I went wrong. Turns out he knew they could be used to stop leaks, he just didn't expect any leaks.

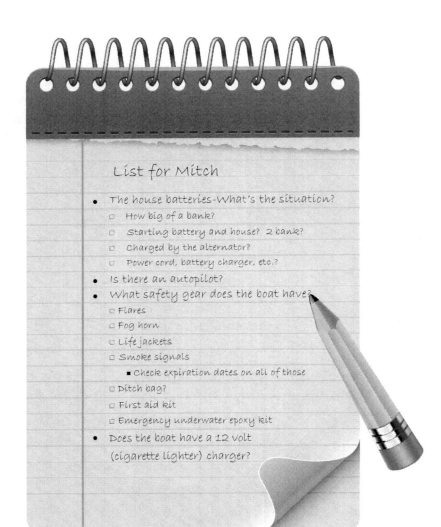

List for Mitch

- The house batteries-What's the situation?
  - How big of a bank?
  - Starting battery and house? 2 bank?
  - Charged by the alternator?
  - Power cord, battery charger, etc.?
- Is there an autopilot?
- What safety gear does the boat have?
  - Flares
  - Fog horn
  - Life jackets
  - Smoke signals
    - Check expiration dates on all of those
  - Ditch bag?
  - First aid kit
  - Emergency underwater epoxy kit
- Does the boat have a 12 volt (cigarette lighter) charger?

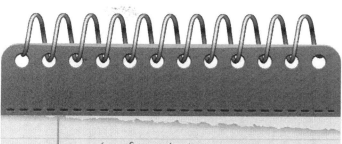

List for Mitch

- Does the boat have a life raft?
- Do all sea cocks function just fine?
  - How many and where–identify and try all
- Dock lines, fenders, etc.?
- Cockpit cushions?
- Make a list of what tools are on board
- Make a list of galley supplies on board dishes-wise-pots, pans, silverware, etc.
- What's the bilge pump situation?
  - How many bilge pumps?
  - Are they wired together or separately?
  - High-water alarm?
  - Check for manual bilge pumps-how many?
- Check for emergency tiller, make sure it works
- Make sure there's wooden plugs, nerf balls, whatever for plugging holes

List for Mitch

- Does the boat have a life raft?
- Do all sea cocks function just fine?
  - ☐ How many and where–identify and try all
- Dock lines, fenders, etc.?
- Cockpit cushions?
- Make a list of what tools are on board
- Make a list of galley supplies on board dishes-wise-pots, pans, silverware, etc.
- What's the bilge pump situation?
  - ☐ How many bilge pumps?
  - ☐ Are they wired together or separately?
  - ☐ High-water alarm?
  - ☐ Check for manual bilge pumps–how many?
- Check for emergency tiller, make sure it works
- Make sure there's wooden plugs, nerf balls, whatever for plugging holes

List for Mitch

- Fire extinguishers?
  - ☐ How many and expiration date
  - ☐ Smoke alarms, CO2?
  - ☐ How many and where?
- Spotlight
- Radio and VHF-check them
  - ☐ Handheld?
- Reef the sails during the sea trial- learn the procedure

"Yeah, Mitch. You can use them to plug a leak."

A moment of silence and then: "But, isn't that what the sea-cocks are for?" Mitch asked, sincerely curious. "Water starts to come in, you just close them, right? That's what they do?"

I was glad he couldn't see my face because I could not hide a smile. That's when I knew it. He had reached stage two. Mitch was knee-deep in denial. I knew because I had been there. When Phillip and I were looking at our Niagara for the first time, I kept looking around the interior for a good bulkhead wall to mount a television on. When I finally showed Phillip the "perfect place" I had found for it—the wall between the saloon and our separate shower stall—I only found one slight hold-up.

"We'll just need to take this lantern out," I told Phillip, all Bambi-like.

"We'll need the lantern," Phillip told me flatly. When my blank stare back didn't convey understanding, he tried another route. "How are you going to power the T.V.?" which was met by an even blanker stare (if that's possible). Then Phillip tried to walk me out of my denial, into the land of the knowing. "Honey, we have to run wires and power it. We need the lantern for light and warmth. I don't think I want a T.V. on the boat."

It turned out he didn't. Neither did I when I finally *understood* what we were truly buying and outfitting—a completely self-sufficient mobile home where we had to engineer a way to generate every bit of light, power, refrigeration and energy needed. I'll be honest, it baffled me when I first learned the two-prong AC outlets on the boat simply would not work when you're on anchor. *They're such a tease!* I thought they would always magically have power at any and all times, just like they do on land. In Innocent Annie Land, boats out on the blue are still connected to the grid.

I was up to my eyeballs in denial. Like me, Mitch was now refusing to believe he had just bought a complete mobile home that sat, at all times, half-dunked in water with the ability to sink.

"You'll want the nerf balls, Mitch, trust me. The sea cocks don't always work."

But that didn't really frighten him either. I truly believe Mitch felt he had purchased the only boat in the world upon which sea-cocks never seized up, because he maintained his stance, renouncing all things possible.

"Well, what about the spares? How many of those impellers and fuel filters and zinc things do I really *need*?"

"However many make you feel comfortable," I told him, thinking a little fear and weight on his shoulders might help give him a little bit of a reality check. *Pssh!* He thrust it off like a rain-soaked jacket.

"Oh, nothing's gonna break twice."

After a while I kind of admired Mitch's euphoric "can do" attitude—as in "my boat can do anything." It was actually nice to *not* have the significant worry and responsibility of making the trip on our own boat. For Phillip and me, the fact that we were embarking on this journey on Mitch's boat made it less stressful and more pure fun. It was also exciting for us to think back through that mental process of rigging out a boat for the first time on an offshore passage. It's a little frightening, a little exhilarating, certainly a fun prospect for adventure. I remembered when Phillip and I wrapped up our own survey/sea-trial and reached that point where it was really happening, we were really about to buy a boat and we were really about to sail her out into the Gulf of Mexico.

After that blissful moment, however, I know there were a lot of lists made, questions asked (on my part), and plenty of talk about fire extinguishers. "The worst thing you can have on a boat is a fire," Phillip had said. I truly think it is his one real fear, which makes it mine by association. But losing the boat entirely, watching it—from the soggy seat of a life raft—roll in heavy seas and sink is the only paralyzing image that haunts me. Those, however, are the nightmares. What lay ahead now for Mitch—and Phillip and me as his willing crew—were the dreams. Crisp visions of the bow slicing through turquoise waters, sunsets spanning an endless horizon, sails taut and pulling us into the wind.

Okay, one sail pulled taut. I could not yet get my head wrapped around that—one sail, the length of the boat, that lowers and raises through the boom. *Through.* I was definitely intrigued by the sail plan on the Nonsuch and was eager to see how she sailed. I'll be honest, I had my doubts about the proclaimed "ease" of it, but I didn't voice them.

It also brought me a kind of secret pleasure to find myself in the position I was in, so soon after becoming a so-called sailor myself. No way was I an expert, but it did feel nice to have experience to pull from. I, at least, knew what half of the things *were* we were talking about this time. During this planning phase with Mitch, he would often turn to me, his face awash with worry, and ask me something about the boat or the passage—whether we should wear life jackets the entire time, what we would do if the GPS went out, etc. Not that I was some seasoned ocean-traveler. Far from it. But between the two of us, *I* was now the more experienced cruiser and I surprised myself at how often I had at least a workable answer.

It was like on-the-job training, though, where you don't realize you've learned how to do something by just watching and going through the motions, until someone asks you to show them how to do it and you just do. When I heard Mitch voice his genuine but sometimes misplaced concerns, it felt pretty cool to be able to easily assuage them. I can definitely see why salty delivery skippers like John Kretschmer like it, not just the passages but also watching novice sailors ask a million questions at first, and then bumble around and get everything wrong on the first try and then, eventually, start to read the wind, trim accordingly and handle the boat like true sailors. I hadn't expected it, but I found great pleasure in passing on knowledge to Mitch that I had proudly earned through experience.

Mitch, however, was not the best student. He would often interrupt, ask a question he had just asked five minutes ago and oftentimes not pay attention the second or third time you answered it. He couldn't help it, though. Mitch was nervous, excited, almost giddy. He prickled with energy every time we talked to him. You could hear it in his voice over the phone. Even before he had set foot on the boat, he was tingling with the idea of buying *this* boat, sailing her back home and then taking her out and dropping the hook in Pensacola's pristine anchorages with his family finally on board. I'm sure he dreamed more about the on-the-hook part than the offshore-delivery part but it was a necessary first step so he was eager to get underway. If the anchoring made him giddy, though, the passage made him nervous.

"Will we have to sleep in our life jackets?" he asked for the fourth time.

"NO!" Phillip and I almost shouted.

It was hard not to at times—shout at him, laugh at him, get pure entertainment out of him. We could tell when we spoke to Mitch after the sea-trial, how much he loved the Nonsuch.

"How did you like the interior?" Phillip asked.

"I could stand up!" Mitch practically shouted, which told us plenty. The fact that big-and-tall Mitch Roberts stepped on this boat and felt, in his words—"comfortable"—was huge.

It seemed it was no longer "too good to be true" at that point, it was just true: a solid, well-made boat in great shape, for a great price, that seemed just about hand-made for Mitch. All that was left was the seemingly little matter of paperwork—letting the time expire for rescinding his offer and then it was final. All Mitch would need to do then would be to bring her home safely across the Gulf of Mexico to Pensacola.

Oh, and to figure out the reefing.

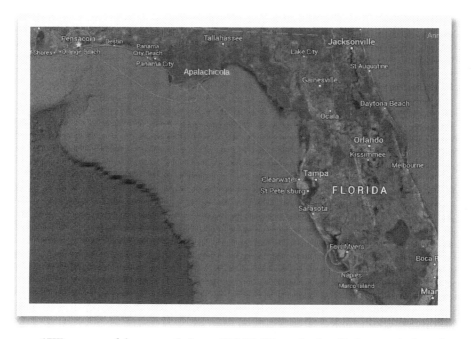

"Were you able to reef the sail?" Phillip asked, a little worried at the thought of sailing a boat with only one sail option: a single sail, all the way up or all the way down.

"Well, yeah, after a while. It's just big and so heavy and I'm not sure which lines go where. I think I need to ..." Mitch trailed off. *I need to work with it some more?* I thought to myself. *Figure out how to sail this huge sailboat I just bought?* No. He was still in denial, remember?

"I need to pick up tennis," he said.

CHAPTER THREE

ANGER

Repeated Irritation at the Repeating Doling Out of Thousands

When the reality of the situation sets in and the affected begins to emotionally connect with what has occurred, anger is often the first emotion to emerge. He may become frustrated with what he perceives as the injustice of the situation.

"**N**ow what is this 'none' stuff?"

"Naan."

"Okay, fine. Naan. What is that? A snack?"

He was big on the snacks.

No surprise here I'm sure. Mitch got the boat, and we got the delivery job. It was kind of an unspoken but settled arrangement when Mitch started seriously considering the Nonsuch down in Ft. Myers. Phillip and I love to sail, we had the requisite offshore experience and we had a debt to pay. The irony of it, though, was almost comical. Not only were the three of us—Phillip, Mitch and I—about to make just about the same trek again on a sailboat, but we were going to do it again on another 1985 model boat and another Hinterhoeller.

"Can you say *Salt of a Sailor,* the sequel?" Phillip shouted when the departure date was finally settled. We were thrilled to embark on another story-worthy Mitch-driven sailing adventure. While we hoped, *this time,* we wouldn't have to hack off any critical parts of the boat, string a puke bucket around one of the crew member's necks, suffer a man down to alleged non-drowsy Dramamine or endure any of the other significant equipment failures we did last time, if we did, we knew it would make for another hilarious sea saga. Plus, we didn't have the worry of it being *our* boat. One of the best passages you can make is one on someone

else's boat.

While we all hoped for a safe and prosperous delivery of Mitch's new boat from Ft. Myers to its new home port in Pensacola, we were also—and maybe this was just Phillip and me although something tells me Mitch maybe a little too—secretly hoping for a bit of an adventure along the way. You don't ever want anything to go wrong during a passage across blue waters, but you know it can always happen. No matter how hard you prepare, plan or tread cautiously, a lot of it's just luck. Sometimes it's just your time for things to go wrong. We didn't want that to happen to Mitch, but if it was going to, we wanted to be there to help Mitch through it and experience and learn from it as well. That was the draw for Phillip and me: the blue water experience.

We set a departure date that worked around everyone's schedule—June 19, 2015—and started planning and provisioning. If everything went well, we expected the entire trip to take seven days but we cleared ten just in case. If there was one (*although there were ten!*) really important things Phillip and I learned from our initial passage across the Gulf it was the most dangerous thing you can have on a sailboat is a schedule. You cannot voyage safely when you're running against the clock. It forces you into weather. A necessary arrival time (unless you need to arrive somewhere to avoid *worse* weather) should never play a factor in your navigational decisions. We learned this the hard way. Have an ETA—or better yet let's call it an HTA (Hopeful Time of Arrival)—but also have a substantial cushion and the understanding that you might get stuck somewhere for days, weeks perhaps, waiting out a storm. If it's a job you're rushing home to, trust me, arriving home safely is worth getting fired over.

We also figured if something did happen and we had to leave the Nonsuch somewhere, we could stage her up for repairs at a port on Florida's west coast, rent a car and drive the rest of the way home to Pensacola. We had to do that with our Niagara on the last leg of her initial passage across the Gulf, so we knew it wasn't the worst case scenario. While we all wanted to see Mitch end his first offshore passage in the Nonsuch by sailing her straight into the Pensacola Pass, we also knew there was the possibility the wind, weather and whatever sailing karma was out there might see otherwise. Whatever the case, we were up for it.

What Mitch was not up for, however, was the provisioning. Mitch was baffled at the amount of stuff Phillip and I put on his list to buy. This was the initial launch of the never-ending chore of buying crap for your boat. *We had warned him, right?* I will say, it is keen fun watching a new friend tiptoe up to the boating ledge. At first he just peeks over out of curiosity. Then he'll kick a little pebble off and watch it bounce and clatter down. Then, before you know it, he's fallen, head-over-heels and tumbles all the way down.

The whole process made me recall mine and Phillip's own flip and tumble. While our Niagara was incredibly capable when we bought her, the more we used her, it was like the *more* we wanted her to be able to do. Cruising is a less-is-more lifestyle, sure, but, I'll tell you, the "less" is only limited by the boat. As boat-owners, we all want our own individual boat to be able to produce as *much* as she possibly can (power, water, ice, speed) and then even a little *more* after that. Cue the Tim Taylor guffaw here. For Phillip and I, it started with solar panels, then we needed a bigger, stronger autopilot, then a new chart-plotter, new instruments, and so on. You'll often hear a marine vendor tell you, "Well, if you're going to go with x, you might as well spring for y." And they're usually right, although it doesn't make the price any easier to swallow. It pisses you off at first, but you just get used to it. After a while, you just shrug your shoulders and break out another thousand. *In for a penny ...* I tried to warn Mitch about this as he was getting ready to fully stock his new mobile marine home.

"You're going to have to buy a lot of stuff in the beginning, Mitch. Then you'll start using all of that stuff and discover what *other* boat stuff you really want. Then you'll have to buy all of that crap too." That's the truth! It's just a process. But when you finally get your boat dialed in— just the way you like it—it's totally worth it. And, after having survived your own tumble, you'll have fun watching friends bump and skip their way down after you, and you'll welcome them heartily to Brokedown Boatsville. I have to admit, I was having a hell of a time watching Mitch.

The naan was the least of his worries. After going through the revised inventory list Mitch made when he was on the boat for the survey/sea trial, Phillip and I made another list of items he would need to purchase for the three of us to safely and comfortably make the passage on the boat and Mitch was angered at the amount of crap he needed to buy for his boat. I saw it bubbling up inside before the fumes ever started to spew out. He had reached stage three: anger.

"Towels? What kind of towels?" he asked, bewildered.

All kinds dude. Dish towels, bath towels, work towels. The three of us are essentially about to move onto your floating home and live there for a week, while we're sailing and working on it. We might need to—I don't know—bathe on occasion, wash our dishes, wipe our hands. I mean, maybe. If you don't think so, though, nix the towels.

He was funny. And some of the costs really put a thorn in his side, like the EPIRB.

"Do we really *need* that?" I remember him asking Phillip.

"Only if you want the Coast Guard to come if we're sinking," Phillip said, trying not to smile.

But I get it. I do. Those little magic haling devices are like $400. It's a jagged little pill going down. But that was just the start of it. If $400 for the EPIRB gave Mitch heartburn, he was really going to take it on the chin with the price tag on the haul-out. There was nothing he could do to stop the bleed.

"So, it's $1,500 to haul out, if need be, for a hurricane?" he was trying to get Phillip to confirm.

"Well, it's $1,500 for the year," Phillip replied.

"Oh, okay, so if they don't haul out, then that carries over for next time, right?"

"No, it's $1,500 a year."

"Even if they don't haul you out?!"

We tried to warn him, did we not?

But I remembered that feeling. When you first buy a boat, it's like you can't comprehend anything but your own catharsis. Dollars flow like angry lava out of you. I recall the "hill charge" was one that angered me when we first hauled out to have our bottom job done.

"So, it costs $400 to haul the boat out, two grand for the bottom job, and then the whole time they're charging you a price per day just to *be* there?" I whined.

"Yeah," Phillip said, slapping me out of it. "It's like the hospital. You can't just stay for free."

Bollucks!

The money-bleed part of boat ownership can be incredibly frustrating. Although Mitch had purchased the Nonsuch for an exceptional price he, thankfully, had a little wiggle room left in his budget, but that doesn't make it any easier to write those checks. He was much more of a good sport about it than I would have expected, though. Mitch really stepped up when it came time to provision. Phillip and I gave him a pretty extensive list of things we would need for the trip— stuff for him to buy, stuff for us to bring and stuff for him to bring, and it was good practice for Phillip and me to go back through that thought process of readying a boat for passage. It was actually fortuitous we had attended a seminar at the Miami Boat Show a few months prior by one of the most famous delivery skippers (*a colorful man, that Kretschmer*) because some of the things he told us he does in preparing a boat for delivery were proving mighty useful now.

One of the things we did that proved very valuable was sort of a happy accident. When Phillip and I started making lists for our own boat delivery, I typed them up on the computer—primarily because I type faster than I write and we could word-search on it if need be to find an item we missed. But, what did that do? Preserved it digitally for all time! This enabled us—when it came time to start provisioning Mitch's

boat—to pull up that old rookie attempt and use it to help fill in gaps of items that we knew were helpful, we just hadn't spontaneously thought of them yet.

It's hard to recall all the systems that could fail and the tools and spares you may need to fix them by memory alone. At least it is for me. A working list of what is needed to outfit a boat for an offshore passage is invaluable. Phillip and I dusted off ours and modified it to suit Mitch's boat and needs. As I scrolled down the list, seeing all of the things I would be using, eating, drinking and likely working on while underway on a sailboat, I got a little tingle. It was exciting to think we would soon be back out there, in the Gulf of Mexico, looking out on a vast body of water with nothing on the horizon but a sun sinking into blue denim.

We went through the list with Mitch, item by item, making sure he

had each one. We checked and double-checked, as had he because he did in fact have everything. Mitch had bought it all, even some extra goodies for the two of us—little treats for us for agreeing to make the passage with him.

"I got the little squirty things for you," Mitch said through a grin, handing me a package of the magic Dasani water enhancers he knew I loved, and perhaps because he knew the water from his tanks might taste as crappy as ours did.

"And, I got some cookies and crackers and Gatorades and candy bars for us," he said to Phillip, all bright-eyed and eager.

Like I said, the man was big on snacks, and he was big on the praise. You could see in his eyes how excited he was for this trip and how

grateful he was we were making the trek with him. The three of us were set to leave the following week and the only thing Mitch got stuck on was the naan.

"It's not a snack. It's bread, like pita. But softer. We'll eat it with the tiki masala."

"The what?"

"Masala. Tiki masala."

"Malasalla?"

"Yeah that. We'll handle that one buddy. See you in a few days. Get some rest."

But did he? No. Mitch called Phillip and me approximately every three-and-a-half hours of those "few days" with a new random question or concern about the trip. We didn't mind though. His enthusiasm and excitement were contagious. He wasn't just excited he bought *a* boat; he was excited he bought *this* boat. You could tell something about this Nonsuch told Mitch she was perfect for him, and Phillip and I were

about to learn why.

It was June 19, 2015 and Mitch, Phillip and I were heading down in a Beverly-Hillbilly style packed-out rental to Ft. Myers to help sail Mitch's recently-acquired 1985 Nonsuch back home to Pensacola. We were sitting in a Panera in Tallahassee, grabbing lunch mid-way through the trip, when we heard it over the loudspeaker.

"Tanglefoot!" she hollered over the loud speaker. I eyed Phillip curiously wondering if he'd just heard what I'd heard or if I was hearing things. "Tangle-FOOT!" she said again, this time with more emphasis on the "foot." Something started to come to shape in the fog of my mind. *It couldn't be?* But it could.

The third time the little Panera chick said it over the intercom Phillip and I started to look around to see who was going to respond. Then we saw him—Mitch—bouncing up to the table with our food trays in hand.

"What do you think?" he asked, looking at us as if his question made sense. Phillip and I kind of sat there dumbly: *What do we think about what?*

"Tanglefoot," Mitch said again. "That's the name of the boat."

You see? It was possibly the only name in the world I could imagine to be *more* fitting for Mitch's boat than "While You're Down There."

"Tanglefoot," Phillip and I repeated him chuckling. I needed a new word for perfect. It was serendipitous, and it wouldn't be long before we would actually be setting foot on the infamous *s/v Tanglefoot.* It was a long haul to make in one day but we got to the docks in Ft. Myers around 10:00 p.m.—just in time for our first Tanglefoot adventure!

The boat was docked in a gated community with water access and slips. Mitch said the owner's broker was supposed to have called the security guards at the gate to let them know he would be coming that day to the boat. Of course that didn't happen and here it was—10:00 p.m.—and we found ourselves being held hostage by the little gated-booth police because we didn't have clearance for admission. Mitch tried calling the broker several times while the gate guards sat there watching him and while Mitch's patience wore thin when there was, time after time, no answer.

"I can't believe these knuckleheads are serious," he told Phillip and me, thankfully behind a rolled-up window so the guards didn't hear. After three failed attempts to reach the broker, he then tried the owner, which I thought was a long shot because it was so late and he was— according to Mitch—"older than molasses," which I guess meant eighty-two. But I'll be the first to admit I was ignorant about the nightlife of eighty year-olds because the owner picked right up, sounding cheery as a nun on Sunday and was able to get us clearance through the booth.

For whatever reason, though—even after getting the thumbs up from the owner—there was still some very important paperwork shuffling and "processing" to be done in the almighty gate booth. You should have seen these three rent-a-goobers, wheeling around on their whirly chairs, shuffling papers back and forth, writing things down like they were solving the mystery of global warming. Mitch kept trying to roll down the window to say something to them—something Phillip and I were sure would get us banned from the place forever—and Phillip kept rolling his window back up to contain him. He was still wallowing around in it. Anger. Because he now had a boat that had to be packed, provisioned and ready for passage the next morning, but these "yahoos" (Mitch's word) wouldn't give him access to it.

Then—in a thinly-veiled effort to interrogate us while the all-important "gated booth processing" procedure was completed—one of the uniformed security blokes came out to chat with us. He pulled his pants up a few times, Barney Fife style and leaned into the driver side window to give us a true Mayberry welcome.

"Evening all," he said tipping his hat to us.

"Evening," we all mumbled back kind of awkwardly, keeping our thoughts to ourselves: *What in the bloody name of gated booths was taking so long?*

"You come here to stay on the boat tonight, huh?"

"Yes, sir," Mitch said back, trying to be patient. I was proud he'd changed the "knucklehead" to "sir."

"What slip are you in?" Fife asked, trying at first to be cordial.

"I don't know," Mitch said, a little embarrassed, but more irritated than anything. *Who gives a crap? Let us in!*

"Well, what dock?" Fife followed up, now a little suspect.

"I don't know," Mitch barked back, now noticeably irritated. "I just know how to get to the boat. I don't know which dock it is."

"Well, there are only *five docks*," Fife snapped, giving us a how-can-you-not-know frown.

"I told you …" Mitch started to fire back and reached for the door handle, his anger seething out. I thought he was about to step out of the vehicle and blow our chances of *ever* getting to the boat that night but, thankfully, he was cut off. Fife No. 2 stuck his head out of the booth, waved some papers in the air and said, "You all have a safe night, now," as the gate buzzed and the arm finally started to lift, allowing us through. The Interrogator hiked his pants up again—because I'm sure there had been some slippage that occurred during the "which dock?" exchange—and gave us a scowl as we drove by. The three of us were laughing about it—now that we had made it through—but those rent-a-Fifes were unbelievable. How important is the documentation of thru traffic in a little gated community in Ft. Myers, Florida? *I mean really?*

Mitch held true to his word. He had no idea what dock the boat was on but he knew exactly how to guide us to it. It was dark and we were worn ragged from the trip but the first sight of her perked us all up. There she was—our home for the next seven days, our carrier across blue waters, *s/v Tanglefoot.* And man did Mitch get lucky! She was a sound, solid, well-built boat. Dirty as all get out but with just a few test swipes of a Clorox wipe I could tell she was going to clean up nicely.

It was also shocking how big the boat felt. At thirty feet, Mitch's boat is a good five feet shorter than ours but it felt five feet bigger in every direction down below. It looked like you could line up three ballerinas in the saloon and have them each do pirouettes and they wouldn't hit each other. I did a few myself to test out the theory. It was indeed a floating condo.

The companionway really blew my mind. The entry-way is like four feet fall, with two measly steps down to the cabin floor. *Two!* Clearance everywhere was incredible. Mitch could stand tall and straight most everywhere in the cabin below.

No wonder Mitch said he felt comfortable on this boat. It was as if it was built for him, or better yet, built *around* him—like those Kohler commercials where the haughty housewife sets a faucet down all dramatically on the architect's desk and says: "Design a home around this." Made me laugh because I don't think a woman like that would carry a faucet in her purse, but it appeared someone had plopped Mitch down at the Hinterhoeller headquarters and said: "Make a boat this man is comfortable on."

The cockpit was massive too. I think the fact that beam of the boat is carried so far forward and so far aft makes it feel so much bigger than ours. The Nonsuch is probably a little squattier—more "fat-bottom girl" than our Niagara—and it can make them a little less comfortable to sail in heavy weather, but it certainly makes them super comfortable to cruise around coastal waters and spend the weekends on. Phillip and I were both really impressed with the layout, look and feel as well as the build and quality of Mitch's boat.

"You done good buddy," I kept saying. "You done good."

We started poking around and tidying things up a bit and discovered some interesting eighty-two-year-old-man finds. There was a complete drawer of canned Buds in the vberth. Think eighteen cans in one drawer and a mounted can crusher by the companionway stairs. The crusher was gross too—all grungy and moldy with years of dirt caked on. That was going to be one of the first things to go. I would see to it. But modifications and thorough clean-up would come later. For now—11:00 p.m. the night before our first offshore passage—it was time to settle in, get all of our provisions on-board and stowed away and the boat put in a somewhat functioning condition for sleeping so we could rise early and make sure she was ready to head out tomorrow morning for the passage. We still had about an hour's worth of work to do just to get all the stuff from rental (*you remember the almighty list!*) on board and our beds squared away before we could crash.

Mitch was so excited showing us around the boat that night he kept dropping things and losing his flashlight. I can't tell you how many times he had to ask Phillip to borrow his.

"Phil, hand me a flashlight."

"Philly, where did that flashlight go?"

After the fourth request, 'Philly' and I decided we were going to have to put a head lamp on him permanently. Or maybe a chest-mounted push light that you could just click on whenever he came near. That would have been helpful.

But you couldn't blame him. Mitch was just excited. This was his boat! His very first sailboat. *Tanglefoot!* And this was his first time to

have friends aboard so he could show her off. And not only would he be showing off her roomy interior, he would soon be showing off her blue water sailing abilities as well. Who wouldn't be excited? That's some pretty good stuff. Definitely worth a couple dropped nuts and bolts and forever-missing flashlight. But I've never seen Mitch so giddy. Since he was all smiles and giggles then, our first night aboard, Phillip and I decided to give him the little Captain's gift we had got him for the passage—a log book for the boat. And I had to throw in an accordion-style waterproof folder for all of his manuals and guides for the different systems on the boat. Pulling from experience, we knew how important it was to keep those handy, dry and organized.

After a couple of hours unpacking, cleaning and stowing, I could tell the boat was starting to give Mitch a new form of grief. His anger had dissipated when we finally made it past the rent-a-guards and began settling in on the boat, but after we made the fourth run from the car and had finished passing all of the stuff on board, assembly-line style, I could see Mitch's mood was shifting when Phillip suggested we open up the engine access panels so we could find and check the fluids.

"Now?" Mitch asked as Phillip hunkered down to begin disassembling the companionway stairs. Phillip's back was turned to Mitch so he couldn't see him, but I could. His arms were hanging low by his sides, his shoulders drooped a good six inches and his britches were hanging low—in need of a good Fife-style hitch-up—but it seemed Mitch didn't have the energy even for that. After a period of silence, Phillip finally turned to look at him and could see what I saw. The man was exhausted.

"Well, just show me where they are," Phillip said, "and I'll check them this time. If they're low, we need to add it to the list for tomorrow."

Mitch lowered himself slowly to his knees, bracing and grimacing on the way down, and finally made it to the cabin floor with a thud as Phillip pulled the stairs back so Mitch could point out the fluid checkpoints.

"Where's my flashlight?" Mitch asked.

CHAPTER FOUR

PHYSICAL DISTRESS

The Squeezing Into of Places in Which You Do Not Fit

As emotions finally begin to take over, the affected may begin to show signs of distress and anxiety. He may feel week, tired and develop ulcers or irregular eating habits as his body is under a great deal of stress and pressure while he is processing the grief.

Mitch's lids were drooping as the three of us sat there talking. It was well after midnight by then; we'd hauled approximately 16.2 loads of crap onto the boat and stowed it away and now—with the fluids checked by First Mate Phillip—it was time to hit the sack. Phillip set to making our double bed out of the starboard settee and I heard Mitch struggling in the vberth.

"Come *on*," I heard him hiss and I perked up an ear. I watched with one eye while I helped Phillip move cushions as Mitch yanked and pulled on his duffel. "Let go!" he pleaded.

I made my way back to the vberth to see what was causing Mitch trouble and had to laugh a little when I saw him, trying to attempt the impossible. During our packing I had tried—as quickly as I could—to assess the various cubbies and lockers on the boat, their size and accessibility and pack them according to priority of the items and their frequency of need. One of the lockers I found might be useful for Mitch's multiple twelve-packs (*yes, multiple*) of Gatorade (after the initial twelve went into the fridge) was a huge cubby on the port side of the anchor locker in the vberth. Not only was the move-about room on the Nonsuch impressive, so was the stowage.

This particular locker was cavernous, and I had accessed it probably five or more times while we had been shoving and stuffing our provisions into lockers that night. Somehow I had managed to shut one of the straps on Mitch's duffel into the locker in the process and he was now so tired, so downtrodden, that instead of crawling onto the bed to free his strap, he was trying to grunt and yank it free sans crawl. That's when I knew our buddy had reached it—stage four: physical distress.

"Lord, give me that," I said, grabbing the duffel from him like a kid snatching a basketball and crawling up on the bed to free his darling duffel from the locker. While I was there I picked up a couple of other things that had made their way onto the bed during our stowing (his foul weather jacket, a sleeping bag and a package of toilet paper) to get them off the bed so the poor man could get some sleep.

"Thanks," Mitch mumbled as he kind of rolled onto the bed, surprising even me by somehow accomplishing the mount without a crawl. I believe it might be better to call this the "wet noodle" phase.

Mitch oozed into the bed and was sleeping before I even shut the vberth door.

Phillip and I chatted just a bit before nodding off ourselves in the saloon. We were planning to make one more provision run in the morning for perishables and then toss the lines around noon to start making our way north, toward either Venice or Clearwater. Venice was going to be a shorter, easier trip—an approximate sixty-five nautical-mile, twelve- to twenty-hour run—and more paralleled to the shore. We were keeping it open as an option in case we suffered some equipment or engine failure or other likely catastrophe on the first leg of the trip. If things were going well, though, we were hoping to make the 125 nautical

mile, twenty- to thirty-six-hour run all the way to Clearwater right out of the gate.

With the air condition going, it felt like Phillip and I were sprawled out in a five-star suite! The sheet was a little stiff—being one of those new items Mitch griped about buying but bought anyway—and the foam was a little hard but my body seemed to sink into them. If I was tired, I knew Mitch was beat. While sleep set in quickly, though, it didn't seem to last. Whether it was the chill or the new sleeping digs or just the excitement of spending our first night on Mitch's boat knowing we were going to sail it out into the Gulf tomorrow, none of us got much sleep that night.

Personally, I blamed Mitch and that darn AC. He has got to cool it (no pun intended) with the air conditioning because that was about the coldest I'd ever been in my darn life. I don't think I will ever be a fan of AC on a boat. It just de-acclimates you. I was tugging and grunting and trying to get every body part covered with mine and Phillip's shared sheet but it still wasn't enough. I was barely groggy and froze-toed when the alarm went off at 5:15 the next morning. The first thing I did was step out into the cockpit to the much-welcomed muggy warmth. It took me a good ten minutes to thaw out topside after our first night on *Tanglefoot*. My feet finally prickled back to life as I walked the dewy deck with a smile. *We're sailing today!*

Mitch must have slept about as soundly as I did because he wasn't long behind me. 5:30 a.m. and the man was up, fiddling with things, looking around again for his flashlight. I'd never seen Mitch up so early but I'd never seen him so excited either. He would ask me a question.

"What was that last thing we needed from the store?"

"Trash bags," I would respond. I already added it to the list."

Five minutes later:

"Oh, here's the list! What was that thing we needed again?"

Mitch was like a kid with a new train set. He couldn't wait to get the track all laid out and watch her go! Except he couldn't find the batteries.

Our plan that morning was to get the dinghy off the davits and secure her on the foredeck. The three of us had learned a hard and expensive lesson the first time we'd crossed the Gulf in our Niagara in not securing our dinghy to the foredeck for offshore passages. There would be no clanging davits this trip, no shearing screws, no hacking off of the dinghy mid-Gulf. Not again. While davits are a convenient, easy way to lower and raise a dinghy on a boat that's cruising around in protected waters, they are not—in my opinion—secure enough to hold a dinghy for an offshore passage. I don't care how heavy duty you tell me they are.

The dinghy that came with the Nonsuch was an eight-foot Walker Bay with a 2.5 horsepower outboard. Although an eight-foot dinghy would generally seem plenty big enough for a thirty-foot boat, for some reason, it still didn't seem big enough for Mitch. But he got in there

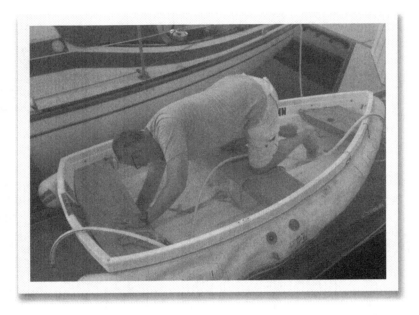

anyway, ass-up, grunting and huffing, and cleaned out the rainwater so we could flip her over on the deck.

At this point I was thoroughly impressed with Mitch. It had been an early rise, with some pretty hefty chores to conquer—all before 6:00

a.m.—and Mitch was taking them all on with a smile, some light-hearted jokes and only the occasional "Now hang on a minute!" So far, he was really stepping up. Until it was time for *him* to check the fluids. While Phillip had done it the night before (more for his own peace of mind and stocking purposes), it is our policy on the Niagara to always check the fluids before you crank the engine. The coolant, the oil, even the transmission. Or perhaps I should say "especially" the transmission, because we check it first. Always.

"Why?" you might ask. Because we seized ours up solid before by not doing it! The first time we made a long passage on the Niagara, we practically broiled our transmission by not keeping her pumping wet with that precious pink nectar. It still kind of baffles us to this day exactly how it happened but it happened and because it did, we now check the transmission fluid before we crank. Every time. And, because it was such a costly and frustrating lesson right out of the gate, this became a policy we did not just suggest to Mitch, we demanded. So, it was his turn now to check the fluids before we cranked that day, starting with the transmission.

I was less than impressed with the engine access on the Nonsuch. It reminded me, yet again, how glad I was that our Niagara is laid out and designed the way that it is—with the easy pull-back sink compartment that allows full-frontal access to the engine and all fluid check-points. To check the fluids on Mitch's boat, we had to access three different, separately-accessed, rather-tight compartments. First, we had to remove the companionway stairs to access and check the transmission fluid on the fore side of the engine.

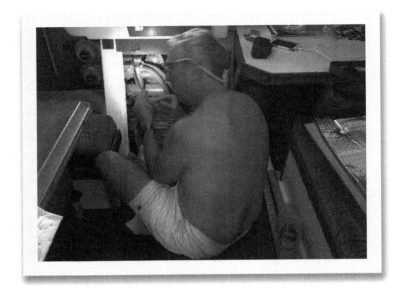

The oil must be checked (not re-filled, mind you, just *checked*), by opening a storage compartment on the starboard side of the companionway stairs and then opening another access door *in* that compartment that allows you to reach the oil dipstick. I felt like Alice in Wonderland walking through all of those doors and shrinking. It was one compartment after another, this hatch then turn left and squeeze through another.

But that's all! *It's not? Tell us more, Bob!* Once you've buttoned up the oil compartment and put the companionway stairs back so you can climb them, you then head up to the cockpit where the coolant bin is located down in the starboard lazarette. It can be checked (not filled) by leaning in upside down and shining a flashlight on it.

"Philly, you got a flashlight?"

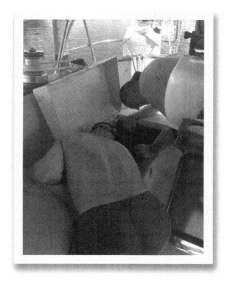

Filling the coolant requires you—or your trained monkey—to go all the way down in the lazarette and sit upright in order to pour coolant in.

Unless, that is, you can pour upside down. I know myself well enough not to attempt that one. While I won't say the access on the Nonsuch was ridiculously *in*accessible, the fluid check-points were a bit tedious, *particularly* for a large man like Mitch. While he and Phillip were checking the fluids, I broke down all of our provisions (taking food and products out of their cardboard boxes and packaging) and took a load of trash up to the marina trash can. That whole process took me about forty-five minutes and when I came back, the boys were still fiddling around in the starboard lazarette. *"He's still checking fluids?"* I mouthed to

Phillip while Mitch's head was down in the hole. Phillip bit back a smile and nodded.

"Which one's the coolant?" I heard Mitch squeal out of the lazarette, which of course meant I had to come look. And there was our 6'4" buddy, wedged down inside of the lazarette. His head was pushed down into his shoulders, his body, twisted and folded, filling every inch of the cubby. And I knew the minute I saw him I couldn't help it. It was practically required.

"While you're down there," I said in my best screechy, mock-Mitch voice as I pointed to the coolant overflow bin.

To my surprise, he actually laughed. Then he nodded his head and rolled his eyes in a *"Yeah, yeah"* manner and began to fight his way out. Knowing he was about to emerge, I stayed in the cockpit to watch the Jack-in-the-Box come out. At first he had two arms out, but his head wouldn't come. Then it was one arm, a shoulder and his head but he was unable to push himself upright. Then it was one open palm in the air and a "Little help, please?"

I grabbed under his elbow and helped ease Mitch out. I knew he had thrown his back out of whack several years back while kite-surfing and I certainly didn't want him to tweak it before we even tossed the lines on this trip. He pulled hard on me, pushed hard on the lip of the lazarette and we finally finagled him out of there. Huffing and sweating and sticking half-way out I could see how much of a real chore that was for him. He sat for a minute on the edge of the seat, his legs still dangling down into the lazarette looking exhausted, his body physically weakened from the exertion. He was really suffering through stage four.

"Like you've been T-boned," her voice came back to me while I watched Mitch, shoulders stooped, sweating, trying to let his body recoup for a minute. "By a Cadillac."

I remembered wondering at the time why, specifically, it had to be a Cadillac, not some other type of car. It was Barbara, the previous owner of our Niagara, and she was warning me when we were readying the Niagara to sail away from her dock what a toll the initial passage was going to take on my body. Her voice came back to me seven days later when we had finally made our own jaunt across the Big Bend of Florida—after a thirty-hour, four- to six-foot seas passage—and that's exactly what my body looked like.

As I had let my own shoulders slump and my own body recoup in the truck stop showers at the Carrabelle marina, I remembered thinking one of the big purple bruises on the bony prominence of my hip looked just like one of those shield-shaped logos on the front grill of a Cadillac. Barbara had certainly been right. My body was beat to hell after that passage. I had to wonder now what was going through Mitch's mind as it was dawning on him how much work this boat was really going to require and what kind of physical strain it was going to put on him.

Tennis lessons probably.

I was sure he'd get quicker at the fluids check over time, but Mitch did impress me by squeezing his 250-pound body into those Wonderland holes—albeit with the requisite grunting, moaning and the occasional "Hang on!" This was, however, just the *checking* of the fluids. We'll get to the filling later.

An hour later and just a shade after 7:00 a.m., the fluids were deemed sufficient and the three of us headed out to make our store runs and grab those "last few items" we had jotted down while inventorying the boat the night before. The plan was ACE hardware for propane and all that kind of trash bag-type stuff (cleaning brushes, sponges, shop towels, dust pan, hand-held broom, etc. along with propane), Publix for our perishable food items and West Marine for some back-up fuel filters. We had planned to grab our store goods and just eat breakfast back on the boat and go. I mean, why else had we hassled Mitch about buying all of that "tortilla-like" stuff the week before?

But it started to become comical when every store we pulled up to (ACE, Target, Publix) didn't open until 8:00 a.m. We deemed it a sign— "Breakfast Break!"—and drove the main Ft. Myers strip a time or two looking for a Starbucks or Bagelheads or something easily recognizable as a standard commercial breakfast joint but, surprisingly, came up empty-handed. Our inability to find a Starbucks in a three-mile radius particularly surprised me. *What kind of Americans are we?* But each time we made a pass we kept eyeing this greasy-spoon diner with a packed-out parking lot and the savory scent of sausage drawing us in.

"Marko's Diner," Mitch read the sign aloud as we finally gave in to the salty scent and pulled into the parking lot. Being a traveler and an adventurer like us, Mitch likes to check out the local stuff when he is in a new place. He wants to eat where the regulars eat, shop where they shop and ask them all sorts of silly questions in the process. It always feels good to support local businesses, too, so Phillip and I were on board. "Marko's it is," we agreed.

I don't know if she was in fact Mrs. Marko but this vivacious, *loud*

Greek woman clad in a shoulder-padded bedazzled sweatshirt—her hair sprayed out on either side in sticky, jut-out wings—was greeting customers the minute the bell on the door dinged. Most folks she greeted by name: "Hey Jim." "Morning Claire." But the newbies you could tell she spotted immediately and really put on a show for them.

"Well aren't you a tall drink of water," she cooed when Mitch walked in.

"That's what they tell me," Mitch said running a hand through some pretend James Dean hair. That was all Mama Marko needed to pull the rug out from under him.

"Is it now? Well I'm glad you're here Big-and-Tall. Have a seat. I'll get you a senior special menu!" she said as she laughed, pulled out one of many Bic pens that lived behind her "hair wings" and nudging her way by him with a pot of coffee in hand.

You have to love a woman who can hold her own, particularly a hefty, big-hearted Greek one. Mrs. Marko was great though, making sure us "out-a-towners" got good service, the whole smorgasbord (eggs, tomatoes, biscuits, grits, gravy) and hot piping coffee. It was just what this motley crew needed to fuel us up for the day. After our Marko's feast, the store runs were quick and expertly executed. The three of us infiltrated ACE then the boys dropped me at Publix while they went to West Marine for the fuel filters. We were back on the boat and packed for passage by 10:00 a.m. With the fluids already checked, all we needed to do was crank and go!

"Be sure to hold it fifteen to twenty seconds," Phillip said to Mitch as he got ready to warm the glow plugs and crank the engine. I was sitting next to Mitch and had to smile as he pushed the button in and started an actual, audible "one one-thousand, two one-thousand" count. He was so careful it was almost cute.

But cute didn't cut it. The engine tried to turn and sputtered a few times but would not crank. Mitch tried three times to no avail. Phillip was worried if he tried to crank one more time without the engine turning over we would pull too much raw water in and it would back up in the engine, so we took a moment to investigate.

I had watched Mitch hold the glow plugs plenty long enough so I knew it wasn't that. Phillip looked at the fuel filter which didn't looked clogged or dirty and the fuel gage read three-quarters of a tank. Then he asked about the starting battery. Mitch had thought it was on, but it was clicked only to "house," not "both." *Aha!* It always takes a little time to learn a new boat. Once that adjustment was made and we gave it a bit more gas she fired right up. The crew let out a collective breath. For a moment, it had seemed our big adventure was about to putter out at the dock.

But she was running great now, purring actually. Mitch was a little anxious about backing out of the dock, but we told him to configure a plan (which lines would be released in what order) and we would execute it. We were there to help Mitch get the boat home, for sure, but we also wanted to let him get as much hands-on, solo-sailing experience as possible because he would essentially be handling the boat on his own once he got her back to Pensacola. So, as often as we could, Phillip and I would have him do everything with us there merely to step in only if he was getting into some real trouble, like training wheels that don't touch unless you start to tip over. Right out of the gate, Mitch got a great lesson in steering his boat in a tight marina.

We wanted to fuel up, pump out and fill the water tanks before jumping out into the Gulf so we planned to stop at the fuel dock. Of course, as luck would have it, there was a line and Mitch had to circle around a few times, back up, pull forward, then turn around again. It even made me nervous seeing all of the maneuvering he had to do. I'm not sure I could have done it. While I am a decent sailor, a great helmsman I am not. It is something Phillip and I know we need to do more—put me behind the wheel. All I can say is it's easy to just play the role you're used to, and Phillip is so good at steering! *Why risk the boat?* I tell myself.

However, right out of the gate, Mitch got a crash-course lesson in tight quarters steering. It was interesting to watch him get a feel for the boat's reaction time. There was a good bit of "easy, gentle, wait for it, slow down!" from Phillip as Mitch leaned a little too hard on the throttle. But with only Phillip's verbal instruction to aid him, Mitch handled the whole three-time turn around and first docking himself.

I set about filling the water tanks and handling the pumpout while the boys fueled her up. The water was no problem. While she did take on a good bit, we got the tanks filled to the brim and the caps secured back down without issue. The waste, however, was another matter.

"I need a hammer," I told Phillip as he walked up on the deck to see what I was struggling with. I could not get the cap off. No matter how hard I turned and groaned and grunted. That one little sliver and a boat key was just not going to cut it. I was starting to imagine what this trip would look like if we started out with a mostly-full holding tank and no way to pump out. While I was sure they had checked the macerator during the survey/sea trial, I would rather *not* be the first one to actually try it out. What if it didn't work? What would we do then? Things could get shitty.

These were the thoughts that were running through my mind as I beat on the back end of the screwdriver, the head wedged into that stupid little sliver when the cap finally clicked free. My guess was the previous owner just never "went" on the boat. I envy the fact that men can easily piss overboard. Or maybe he never pumped out at the dock because it felt like the waste cap had not moved in a decade. Luckily, though, she finally spun free. We took a load off and so did I. *Whew.* While I was glad to help Mitch sail his boat back to Pensacola, I was secretly hoping that offer would not have to include head repair or maintenance. It was just a hope, though, not an ultimatum. When you sign up as crew for a trip like this, it's an unspoken offer to wear any hat necessary: sailor, mechanic, electrician, even plumber.

Once we were emptied out and topped off, we shoved off the dock and I started to feel that excitement that always builds in me when I see the Gulf on the horizon. It is, currently, the only body of blue water I have sailed in, but she is still vast and churning, and full of her own challenges and awe-inspiring sunsets. I could see her, big and blue just outside the Pass and I was anxious to get to her, but I forgot who I was traveling with. Mitch can't leave any place without stopping to talk to somebody first.

"Hey!" a sailboat named *Miller Time* shouted at us as we passed them on starboard just before entering the pass.

"Hi!" Mitch shouted back, not curious at all as to why they were saying hello to him. *Everyone should say hello to me*, his smile said.

"Is that Wade's boat?" *Miller Time* asked, referring to the previous owner, Mr. Eighty-Two.

"Oh, yeah! It is!" Mitch hollered back excitedly. "I just bought her!" he beamed.

"Oh, congrats!" *Miller Time* shouted back. "Have a great trip."

Mitch was looking at Phillip, then at me, then back to Phillip with this silly, open-mouth grin. *Did you see that? Did ya?* His goofy face inquired. He was a small-time celebrity already. It was clear Mitch was

going to get a lot of looks in his big-stick cat rig, and he was totally loving it.

Once we made it out of the channel Phillip decided it was high time we threw up the big-ass sail on the Nonsuch. That man does not like to motor. I stationed myself at the mast, pulling the halyard manually, while Phillip set up on the winch and Mitch held the wheel. While it was difficult to pull by hand at first, it was moving along until we got to the reef points. Unfortunately, the last time the boat had been sailed—during the survey/sea-trial—they had practiced reefing her to make sure all the lines worked properly. That meant the sail was still reefed as we were trying to raise her which always makes it tougher. Our first time raising the sail, we got a crash course on the reefing lines, which one was reef one and reef two as well as their particular hang-ups and pinch points. Once we got all the reefing lines loosened, though, we still had another three or four feet to go to fully raise the sail to the top of the mast. That's when the real fun began.

I was pulling the halyard down at the mast while Phillip was cranking on the winch back in the cockpit, but I had done all I could do on my end. The rest of the sail just had to be muscled up using the winch and—*my God*—that thing shrieked and cried with every turn. I watched as the halyard grew tauter and visibly thinner before me. I gave it a light tug a time or two to see if it still had some bend but after five or six cranks on the winch it wouldn't budge at all. It was as tight as a steel cable and we still had another two or so feet to go at the top of the mast.

I hollered to Phillip to keep cranking and the winch continued to wail. I didn't dare touch the halyard after that. I thought just my light fingers on it and the whole thing might explode. I couldn't stand the sight or sound of it anymore. I backed away from the mast and just stood near the cockpit, my hands ready to come up and protect my face if there was an all-out halyard explosion. Mitch was watching from the helm, staring at the top of the mast to see when the sail finally made it to the top. "Keep going," he shouted to Phillip who looked to me topside for confirmation.

"It's still got some bag in the bottom, but who cares?" I shouted to Phillip, a little nervous to push the rigging any further right out of the gate. We've got plenty of sail up."

I was not in any way inclined to blow a halyard our first time raising the sail. I was literally afraid to go anywhere near the mast with that much tension on the halyard. We had squealed her to her limits. Phillip gave it just one more crank and said, "That's good." Mitch looked up through the bimini window and started to say something but I heard Phillip's voice over whatever he tried to mutter out: "It's good."

Thank God, I thought. This may sound silly, but it's the truth. Raising that sail was frightening. It took me a few hours before I would approach the mast again without my hands poised, ready to cover my face. But it was now up and we were finally sailing! Motor-sailing, but that still counts, and making 6.2 knots our first run into the Gulf.

Phillip and I were surprised the boat pointed as well as it did. I guess with the massive surface area of the sail that the wind has to travel around, it's got more suction into the wind than you would think. Also—just as Mitch had predicted—tacking the boat was astonishingly easy. What do you do? You turn the wheel. That is all. The sail handles the

rest. Not that letting the genny out on one side and cranking her in on the other side—like we do on our sloop rig boat—is super exhausting, but it can be a bit of a chore in heavy winds or when you're trying to kick back, eat grapes and read a book. Occasionally—when I'm sunk in deep in a riveting chapter—Phillip's cheery "Time to tack!" is met with an audible groan.

On the Nonsuch, though? You just turn the wheel. That's it. You could tell Mitch was getting a real kick out of that. He tacked far more than he needed to that morning just because he was having such a good time doing it. It was fun to watch him enjoy his new boat, though. We had a nice day motor-sailing. The sea state was calm and smooth. It would have been perfect for sailing had the wind not been right on our nose. For that reason, we kept the iron sail going to make headway but even with the motor running, we were only making 3.8 knots trying to tack back and forth into a light headwind.

We were still debating whether to point toward Venice for a shorter run or just push on through to Clearwater. With the motor running solid and the sail and rigging all fairly tested and proving seaworthy, the crew decided to just keep trucking to Clearwater. Everyone was in good spirits and enjoying the passage so far. Wanting to capitalize on our fresh morale and cover a good bit of a ground during our first offshore passage, we decided to drop the canvas so we could point straight toward Clearwater and chug it out under motor.

"Hang on," Mitch shouted. "Move!"

He and I were topside dropping that big Nonsuch sail for the first time and it was not pretty. If she's got the slightest wind in her, she topples all over the place. Half of her fell outside of the boom on the port side. I was trying to push her back in and Mitch was trying to push me out of the way. One more "Move!" and I was going to push him right off the boat. I knew he was trying to be chivalrous and all, but if I can do it, let me do it. I'm not a die-hard feminist. I'm just occasionally capable. *So you move!*

When it came to the tail end of the sail—the clew—though, I was not, unless I climbed up, one awkward toe on the stern rail, and laid my body weight across that big, square bimini. Just standing on the coaming, the sail was literally out of my reach. I let Mitch handle the back end of the sail while I went forward to wrestle the mammoth we had piled up there. After some false starts and head-scratching, Mitch and I finally came up with a hug-and-snug maneuver (patent pending) where he would wad up an armful of sail, hug and lift it, and I would snake the sail tie around and tie her down.

"Did you get it?" Mitch asked in a huff as I tried to pull the sail tie around the largest part of the sail near the mast. *You'll be the first to know when I do*, I was thinking, but I said nothing because I almost had it. The wadded-up body of the sail barely fit in Mitch's pretty impressive arm span as he was hoisting it up so I could get under, and I could see in his face the pain he was trying to hold back. *Still enjoying stage four I see?*

And that sail. *Sheesh*. Have I mentioned before how big that sail is? We put approximately ten sail ties on her, from mast to stern, then came the job of putting the sail cover on. Again after a few false starts, snaps and the occasional "I got it!" we finally figured out it was easier to roll that thing down the length of the sail, from mast to stern, in order to put her on and then roll it up, from stern to mast, like a giant burrito to stow her away. The sail cover is also best applied using the hug-and-snug maneuver referenced previously. I seriously did think about writing a comical technical manual for Nonsuches on this trip. I guess this is it.

Once the sail was secure, Phillip throttled the engine up and we were making five knots due north toward Clearwater. On that heading, we were set to reach Clearwater the following afternoon so talk turned to divvying up the night shifts. On the first passage the three of us had undertaken together years past, we had decided on two-hour, two-on/ one-off shifts. Meaning, one crew member held the wheel, one crew member was on watch while the remaining crew member rested for two hours, then we would rotate. It worked well until we lost one crew member to debilitating seasickness—I won't name names (*Mitch!*)—at which time Phillip and I eased into a one on/one off rotation out of sheer necessity.

I was still shamefully new to sailing at that time so the brunt of the helm-holding fell on Phillip. However, when Phillip and I sailed our boat the following year down to the Florida Keys and back, we both held true one-on/one-off, two-hour night shifts and found it worked well. So we decided this time—with a crew of three—to do one-on/two-off shifts to allow the crew more rest, feeling Mitch could likely handle a solo shift just fine. I mean he had to. It was his boat.

It was going to be nice this time to get at least one, solid four-hour stint of sleep. The first and last shifts (8 to 10 p.m. and 6 to 8 a.m.) we called the "gravy shifts" because everyone is usually up with you during those times so you're not really alone at the helm. Phillip wanted to take the short straw this first leg of the trip and get his two-crap-shifts night over with right out of the gate. Looking back on it, it was a smart move—take the worst leg while we were all still fresh and excited on our first passage. But Phillip must have played us well, because Mitch and I happily signed up for one gravy shift and only one solo shift during the night. *Yippee!*

With that settled and entered into the log book (so there could be no debate later), we decided to put the bimini down and enjoy the sunset from the cockpit. While I prefer the Niagara, hands down, to the Nonsuch, the ability to easily drop the bimini was pretty sweet. It is a rather large bimini, which does mean great shade protection, but it

Night Shifts

Me: 8 p.m. - 10 p.m.

Phillip: 10 p.m. - 12 a.m

Mitch: 12 a.m. - 2 a.m.

Me: 2 a.m. - 4 a.m.

Phillip: 4 a.m. - 6 a.m.

Mitch: 6 a.m. - 8 a.m.

also makes you feel a little claustrophobic and caged when it's up. Once it drops, however, it's like stepping out of a tent into the crisp night air above you. It really connected us with the environment. We watched the sun turn into a hot pink ball on the horizon. I love when it does that—blazes so bright you can hardly look at it but you can't look away either—as it drops down beneath a denim blue horizon. She put on a stunning show our first night out there.

Phillip and I cooked up a hot batch of red beans and rice and salad for dinner and dished out some hearty portions for the crew. We watched Mitch curiously, though, as he merely pushed a few beans around, ate a sprig or two of lettuce and then said he was full. He was definitely exhibiting some strange eating habits, another unfortunate side effect of stage four. Mitch was a big guy and he usually had no problem putting

away big portions of food. Now he was cutting beans in half and trying to stomach them down. We didn't want to say it (because sometimes just saying it makes it happen) but we suspected Mitch's body was not taking well to this passage. We worried he was getting seasick. Again.

Unfortunately, during our first offshore passage with Mr. Roberts he got monstrously seasick and was put down for twelve hours after taking some so-called non-drowsy Dramamine. While I have heard seasickness is one of the worst feelings you can possibly have (thankfully I have no first-hand knowledge of this) it was tough on the remaining two-member crew to take up his slack for such a long period of time. Phillip and I were hoping, for our own sakes—so we wouldn't have to man the helm as much—that wasn't happening this time. We didn't want to say it, though. It's like a jinx. We just asked: "You getting tired, buddy?"

"Yeah. Tired," Mitch said, seemingly thanking us for the courtesy pass and taking it straight to bed. "I'm just going to rest up for my shift," he said as he headed down the companionway stairs. Rest is definitely what that man needed. Over the course of the last twenty-four hours, he had pushed his body through a massive provisions haul, complete stowing and organizing of the boat, a rather pitiful fight with a duffel bag, and an exhaustive circus act this morning checking the fluids.

"Get some rest, buddy," Phillip and I both said as Mitch headed down below. We were hoping we weren't going to lose him again to seasickness, but if we were, I certainly wanted to be fueled up for a more trying, two-person-only offshore trip. I grabbed his unfinished bowl of red beans and rice and scarfed it.

Phillip sat up with me during my first night shift from eight to ten.

You see? Gravy. We were breathing and basking in the serenity of being back out on blue waters with an unfettered horizon and cool night air setting in. *God it felt good.* But, just as she starts to sense you getting all comfortable and cozy, she likes to remind you who's in charge. Right after the sun dipped we heard an ominous rumble behind us. Phillip and I turned around to look out from the stern and saw big, rolling thunderheads on our horizon. I was glad Mitch was sleeping so he couldn't see what was coming up on his boat and crew.

"We better put the bimini back up," Phillip said, "in case the storm comes."

CHAPTER FIVE

GUILT

The Short-Lived Instinct to Apologize for Your Boating Lifestyle

*The affected may feel guilty or somehow responsible for the events
that have transpired. He may blame himself for what has happened
and feel heavy with the burden of responsibility.*

"Annie." I felt a jolt. "It's your shift," he said over the Velcro of his jacket stripping off and his footsteps clomping back to the vberth. I blinked a few times trying to orient myself and cranked my head immediately to the cockpit to find an unmanned helm. "Auto's on," I heard Mitch say as he plopped onto the bed in the vberth.

"Oh, and Phillip's on next," he was sure to remind me. *Why thank you.*

I guess having sailed with Phillip for so long there are just some routines, some mutual unspoken courtesies that we fell into that Mitch apparently wasn't privy to. But I guess that's our fault. This was his first offshore passage with solo night shifts and we didn't tell him. When Phillip or I approach a shift change, we generally go rouse the man coming on about ten minutes before our shift is over to give him time to wake up, get some water, and brush his teeth. Or hers, I suppose. Whatever it is he feels he needs to do to feel fresh and alert for his shift. Then we usually sit together at the helm for a bit, discuss the conditions, give a report of any notable events, sightings or observations and fill out the cruising log together (the time for which usually corresponds with the shift change). In general, we just have a routine of helping ease one another from dead sleep to alert watchman. It's not anything Phillip and I talked about or planned out; it was just a pattern we fell into.

But Mitch? Man how I wish he'd had the shift after me. I would have loved to have woken him in the same fashion: "Hey, buddy! Snap to. The helm's unmanned. Get up there!" But, technically, he had every right. It was my shift. My turn to hold watch. I needed to get up there. In the grand scheme of things, it really was a minor transgression. Mitch had held his first solo shift—without complaint—and had done a good job of it, his very first offshore passage, from Ft. Myers to Clearwater, Florida, on *s/v Tanglefoot.*

It didn't take me long to ease into the atmosphere in the cockpit. It was so crisp in the Gulf, the moon lighting every little chop, like the water was pulsing with energy. The stars were so clear against the black sky. When you're out on the water they don't have to compete with any man-made light. It's like everything is clicked into high definition. A view that was once hazy is wiped crystal clean and you can then see that all of the stars you could see on land actually have fifteen equally bright stars between them and five more little sparkling ones between each of those. It seems impossible to find a patch of pure black.

I wish we could have dropped the bimini that night but we still had the storm on our stern that threatened rain. While the bimini on the Nonsuch drops fairly easily, raising it is at least a two-person job and not something Phillip, rightfully, thought the crew should be doing in the middle of the night, potentially in the thick of a storm. It was the right call, but I would have loved to have sailed that night without the bimini. I was hoping that would happen at some point on this trip.

I also hated that we were still motoring but the wind was still so light—blowing maybe five knots—right on our nose it would have taken us three days to sail to Clearwater. The motor on the Nonsuch was chugging right along, though, impressing us all. And Mitch was blessed with a powerful beast-of-an-autopilot on the Nonsuch. Mounted beneath the floor of the cockpit—steering the wheel with a heavy-duty hydraulic arm—that thing held in twice the weather as the little belt-on-the-wheel autopilot Phillip and I have on our Niagara. We had already been talking about upgrading our autopilot the year prior but this trip on Mitch's boat served as a stark awakening that we needed to stop talking and just do it already.

The autopilot on the Nonsuch was our champion on the trip. With the autopilot and the Westerbeke purring right along, the first hour of my shift was pretty easy. The second, however, began with a startling crack. I had just written the heading on the log book page when I saw it out the corner of my eye.

Lightning is beautiful. It really is. When it's far away and you can just watch it and wonder about the illusive static forces that are causing such shocking white streaks in the sky. Just wondering how it occurs is fun. Wondering whether it's going to spark out of the sky and strike your boat, however, is not. When I turned in for my first sleep shift around 10:00 p.m. that night, the lightning storm had been just that: beautiful and far away. Mid-way through my 2:00 a.m. shift at the helm, it started clocking around our port side and getting closer.

Every once in a while I would see a crack of lightning out of my peripheral on the left, then 'every once in a while' became every few minutes. With only the iron sail pushing us along, we had pretty much free reign over what direction we wanted to go. I picked the one that would take us *away* from the lightning storm and shifted us over about thirty degrees east to try and head away from it. I hated to take us off course but if there was a lightning storm on our previous heading, an earlier arrival time was a sacrifice I was more than willing to make to avoid a storm. When I roused Phillip around 3:45 a.m.—*with* the obligatory ten-minute wake-up routine—I let him know the status and he remained on my east heading as I fell back into the dead zone around 4:00 a.m.

Thankfully, it seemed the Gulf just wanted to toy with us that evening, because the lightning storm never fell on us. Not that night. The crew woke to still waters and a stunning sunrise off the starboard side the next morning with an ETA of late afternoon in Clearwater.

Mitch seemed to be faring pretty well. Whatever queasiness had

come over him the night before seemed to have subsided. It was interesting when we talked about the night shifts to see what different emotions and reactions the crew had to the conditions. Mitch told us with the lightning storm threatening us from the stern and only the chugging engine capable of pushing us to safety, he was a little worried, a little scared, which was justifiable. If the engine quit for whatever—a hundred totally possible reasons—we wouldn't have been able to sail away from that storm with the light wind on our nose. The engine was our only ticket to safety.

"It's not like we're in swimming distance," Mitch said, sort of fumbling with the figure eight knot on the end of the main sheet. "And we couldn't drop anchor." Then I could sense it coming. He was easing out of stage four and into stage five: guilt. "I kept wondering if I remembered how to use the EPIRB and I knew I didn't. Philly said there was some antennae thing I flip up and then another thing to flip over and then a button but what if ..." his voice trailed off.

It was kind of strange for me to comprehend, knowing Phillip and I had so vigorously signed up for this passage and now Mitch was feeling guilty for bringing us out there. I think his first night shift frightened him more than I thought it would and—with a heart the size of Texas like his—it made him feel terrible to think, by bringing us along on this passage with him, he had inflicted that kind of terror on us. For the first time Mitch realized his little boat was miles away from shore, two of his best friends were on it and our safety was undoubtedly in her hands.

"What if we sail this boat right on home, huh?" Phillip piped up, clearing Mitch's little black fog in the corner. "With the wind we have right now, we could turn her toward Pensacola and get on a nice beam reach!" Phillip said excitedly. And that was about all he had to say. He wanted to remind Mitch that we were happy to be on this trip with him. Even if there were times when we were tired, a little uncomfortable, or ready to get off the boat, we knew those times would be followed by others when we were mesmerized by a lightning show off the stern or leaned over the toe-rail exhilarated by the water lapping by. Phillip and I had signed up for it all, voluntarily, and whatever happened along the way was in no way Mitch's responsibility. It seemed Phillip's boisterous comment and slap on Mitch's back conveyed that and snapped him out of his guilt funk—for the moment at least—because Mitch chippered up, smiled and patted the fat coaming around the cockpit, saying, "You got this *Tanglefoot*."

She had proven herself steady and true, too, chugging us right through the night, away from the storm and into a beautiful streaking sunrise. It had been a slightly frightening but also awe-inspiring first night on passage. The only bummer was the motoring but that engine was solid as a rock. Never a hiccup, never an issue (that wasn't a result of operator error). Thankfully, the breeze freshened up around 9:00 a.m. and we decided to drop the bimini and hoist the huge ass Nonsuch sail (again with the same halyard yelp and threat of explosion). Despite her persistent squealing, we were able to get her cranked up and were

finally able to sail without the engine, for the first time since the previous morning.

While it is physically and technically not that mind-blowing—you tie a sheet to a stick hoisted on a raft and it will push you along—there is something about being on a boat and watching it move through a vast body of blue water by the sheer power of the wind that is soothing. It sparks a calming at-oneness with the world around you. We all kicked back in solace and just appreciated what the boat was doing. Sailing. Finally. Connected with the salt air and sky.

Sadly, it didn't last long. If I said the breeze was fresh around 9:00 a.m., I would have to deem it stale and a little flat by noon. Like a four-day old liter of soda that opens with no fizzle. And, without the wind, it was scorching under the hot, overhead sun. We knew we were going to have to re-crank but Phillip wanted to check the fluids before we turned the engine over again.

All told, she had been running a little over twenty-four hours straight through the night before we had shut her down that morning. Having experienced a rather unfortunate engine failure on our own boat because of lack of fluids after a solid thirty-hour run, Phillip and I were a little sensitive about the fluid situation. Again we made Mitch do most of the heavy lifting in checking all the fluids to be sure he knew how to access each one and identify issues.

And while all three—transmission, oil and coolant—are located in three separate areas on the boat and I'm not saying I could check them all in under five minutes, I don't think it would take me the better part of an hour! A short thirty-five minutes later (*which was an improvement!*)

Mitch had checked them all and deemed us ready to re-crank and carry on.

It seemed, however, the task was a bit taxing on him. By the time he had wrestled the companionway stairs back on and trudged up them into the cockpit, he was a heaving, sweating mess and it seemed the sticky chore had inspired a new idea in him. One that made him forget his current endeavor and move right on to the next, not uncommon for Mitch. As soon as he had clipped the stairs in, but before he had screwed in the wing nut to secure them, he bounced up to the cockpit to share his bright, shiny idea with Phillip.

"Just one at a time," I heard him say to Phillip as I was screwing in the nut on the stairs, which made me perk up. *One at a time to what?* I thought, a little worried what scheme our buddy had freshly-concocted for the crew. "And just for a minute," Mitch said, his shoulders shrugged, his face pleading.

"Let's go for a dip!" Mitch squealed.

Phillip and I eyed each other, likely wondering if the other was actually considering this. Aside from all of today's fancy EPIRB, life jackets, tethers, etc., there are really only three primary safety rules when boating: 1) stay on the boat; 2) keep the boat afloat; and 3) don't run into anything. *This was rule number one!* But that's precisely what Mitch was proposing.

With the state of things—the glaring sun, beautiful beckoning turquoise waters around us, no current or wind to speak of—I couldn't say that I was opposed, but I was kind of bewildered. You exert so much effort during offshore passages trying to stay *on* the boat—running jack lines the length of boat, buying and wearing fancy, hydro-static inflatable life jackets, attaching yourself with jaws-like clips to the boat everywhere you go—and here was Mitch, suggesting we just jump off!

But Mitch was standing there with lakes of sweat drooping down from each armpit as well as his neck. I think the thought of what he would smell like later swayed me, but I didn't speak first. Plus, looking out at the crisp green water dancing by, part of me just liked his novel idea. We might get some flak for this. All I can say is it felt like the right decision at the time.

"Let's tie a few safety lines first," Phillip said, to my surprise and delight. "And only one in the water at a time." I eagerly started fishing around in the port lazarette for some lines to tie off the stern. But, while the order wasn't discussed, *i.e.*, who would go first, I think we all knew who was going to jump overboard first anyway. Yet I also knew—even if I *did* point that fact out—he would say: "Well, it was my idea!" I just know the man. It wasn't two seconds after I had a line tied off, trailing behind us that I heard him hobbling up on deck.

"Man overboard!" Mitch hollered as he launched off the toe rail and attempted a lopsided cannonball.

Phillip and I watched greedily as Mitch shook fresh, cold water from his head and splashed around a bit. While it did not seem there was a current, Phillip noted we were still doing 1.8 knots with no sails and no engine. Mitch was struggling a bit to keep up with the boat and struggling as well to find the safety line. We told him to tie it to himself so we wouldn't lose him and the man decided his foot was as good a place as any.

"Tanglefoot!" Mitch shouted from behind the boat; his foot snagged in the line, the boat dragging him along. I can only imagine what the boat thought of him then as her new owner.

Phillip, ever the gentleman, let me plunge after Mitch emerged. *My God the water felt good.* It was like it seeped into your pores the minute you splashed. All of the sweat and sunscreen, the oil and muck were washed away. It was strange but stimulating to feel my hands cool and wet on my face. I wiped them up and down on it probably a dozen times during that two-minute swim. It was just the refresher we all needed. I also used the swim break to rinse our breakfast dishes and the French press from the coffee, which was much easier to do overboard and helped preserve water. Mitch decided a second plunge was in order while I was rinsing the dishes and I had to do a double take when I looked back, sure the current had sucked his britches clean off!

Part of me laughed at myself, though, for looking back twice. *Is that a sight you really want to see, Annie?* I think it was instinct more than anything, but I could have sworn Mitch was bottomless out there. Or so it seemed. His trunks under water were just about the distinct color of his bare bottom. *Don't ask me how I know the color of Mitch's bottom but I do.* But I would not have put it past Mitch, losing his drawers out in the Gulf. I was pleased to see his trunks, though, when he climbed back up the swim ladder. Once we had all crew and their britches aboard, we piled back in the cockpit—now feeling and smelling and heck of a lot better—cranked the engine and set our sights on Clearwater, eager for some shore-leave.

Stepping down into the cabin, however, feeling—for the first time on the trip—fresh and squeaky, I suddenly realized how gunky and dirty the boat felt. We had yet to undertake the necessary Simple Green and elbow grease I had mentioned when we first saw the pictures of the boat that we knew would bring her back to life. Motoring along with not much else to do, I decided it was high time to set my radar on mold and dirt and set to it, albeit with something a little stronger and more magical than Simple Green.

I'm not really sure when my love affair with Magic Eraser began, or how it started. I wonder if it has anything to do with the resemblance between that sexy bald man on the package and my very own Captain.

Whatever the reason, I fell hard for that magic man. He erases anything! Red rim from the wine bottle on your white countertop? Gone. Rust stain on your cockpit floor? Never happened. Black scuffs on the decks? Disappeared. Magic Eraser rocks. It just does. The pope should use it to daub the heads of parishioners and wash away their sins!

The last few hours we were underway toward Clearwater I busted one of those magical white blocks out and went to town on the cabin of Mitch's Nonsuch. The interior really was in such great shape. Structurally at least. Was it moldy, dirty and grimy? Yes! It was filthy. But did the Magic Eraser fix all of that? Of course!

A little elbow grease and some magic and the Nonsuch looked like a completely different boat down below a couple hours later. We had spent most of our time during this initial passage inspecting and learning the systems, hoisting the sail for the first time, trying the reefing lines, checking the fluids of the engine, etc., but once we felt all of the primary systems were running fine, it felt nice to finally get in there and do some cosmetic work. While you always want your boat to run and perform well, making her *look good* is high on the list as well. I wiped just about every surface below with some concoction of bleach and magic, most of which was expended on our little royal marine throne.

Things went south when I got to the head. Usually, it's common courtesy on a boat to put the lid on the head back down when you finish your business. It's always possible things can go to tumbling or be dropped when underway and the black hole at the bottom of the toilet is not where you want them to fall, particularly a toothbrush. Everything had seemed to be working fine with the head during our first passage

but when I lifted the lid this time to give her a thorough scrub, I found a nice little brown pond awaiting me at the bottom of the bowl. The holding tank was backing up into the bowl. *"Hooray!"* said my inner Misses Clean.

Then memories of the gifts Mitch left in the bowl on our boat after we fed him "broccoli crappola" and I debated shutting it back down and acting like I'd never seen it. *Out of sight, out of mind ... till Mitch finds it.* But I knew we still had five, six, maybe more days left on this trip and I didn't want to spend each one cringing at the thought of lifting the lid. I was sure the joker valve on the head was failing and allowing about three inches of holding tank goodness to eek back into the bowl and slosh around for the ride.

I debated telling the boys so Mitch could handle it underway, but I honestly was worried his potential fiddling with it might make it worse.

At least it was just an inch of brown goodness right now, I thought to myself. *What if he turned a few screws the wrong way and it started over-flowing onto the floor?* I decided it was just easier to dump a little bleach in and let that temper the sight and smell of the sewage I had been met with. Now the crew was just faced with a little pool of brown bleach every time they lifted the lid. That wasn't so bad.

Aside from the wayward joker, the boat was cleaning up extraordinarily well. Mitch had found a real gem. With still unfavorable wind (light and right on our nose) we were still motoring, which made the clean-up job a bit of a sweaty endeavor in the stuffy cabin. *There goes that crisp Gulf freshness.* This time it was going to be me who was stinking up the place later. For my benefit, as well as the crew's, I was definitely aiming for a nice, refreshing shower in Clearwater.

After all of the motoring we had been doing, we definitely needed some fuel too, so we pointed Mitch in toward the fuel dock at Clearwater. Only his second time docking and, I have to say, he did a pretty good job. The man loves that throttle though. I don't think he realizes how fast he is really going because he tends to barrel in. It was clear the team was going to have to work on this. And we tried! When Mitch was making his way from the fuel dock into the transient slip for the night, Phillip kept trying to ease him back: "Slower, buddy. Slower than *that*!" But Mitch was still flying into the slip with Phillip and me trying to catch pilings to slow us down.

"Mitch!" Phillip shouted back to the cockpit.

"I'm not giving her any gas!" Mitch shouted back. Cue Annie frown here.

Thankfully, we had a few dock hands come up to help us and they held the bow off the dock but I'd have to give Mitch a B- on that one. When we got her tied off and secure, Phillip walked back to the cockpit, looked at Mitch, pointed to the shifter and said: "Neutral. Reverse."

It's easy to forget if you don't drive a sailboat often. It's not like a car where you can just step on the brakes. You don't have brakes on a boat but you do have options. If you're going too fast, even in idle, you can throw it in neutral to slow her down or reverse and throttle her up a little if you need to really slow her down. I guess you could call those "sailboat brakes." After a docking lesson or two and a few gentle reminders from Phillip, Mitch started to do this on his own. It just takes a little time to train your brain. But he is still heavy on that throttle. Don't ask me why. I think it's his antsy nature. He's too impatient to go slow.

Once we got the boat secure, we gave her a nice rinse down and the crew immediately set their sights on a shower. I was coated in salt, sweat and Magic Eraser filth. It was still a steam bath outside and we were all sweltering walking toward the showers, dreaming of that first icy drench. However, the swelter outside could in no way compare to the sauna inside.

The air conditioning was out in the women's bathroom and it felt like a muggy one hundred degrees in there. I had to kick and flail out of each sticky scrap of clothing I had on. While the water was cool, the minute I stepped out of the stream, I started sweating again. I mean the very minute. The thought of dressing in there seemed absurd. Whatever I did in there, I'm not sure you could call it a shower. Maybe a sauna rinse? A steam spray? I was nowhere *near* clean when I came out. My clothes, already drenched, were clinging and sticking to every part of my body. My face and brow had already beaded up and was dripping by the time I got decent enough to emerge.

Only because I didn't think a nude streak to the boat would have been appropriate did I dress in there. Mid-June, in the middle of Florida, and it was cooler outside than it was in that blasted shower room. I was at least soothed by the discovery that the men's bathroom suffered from the same AC dilemma. The crew all had a good time regaling our individual streak contemplations and sweaty dressing struggles. Funny, each of us had unilaterally decided to brush our teeth and hair (well, those who had hair) and do all of that post-shower potions-and-lotions stuff back on the boat. We had all half-dressed, hugged our pile of bath crap to our chests and bolted back to the boat.

Why? Because there was definitely one place in that marina where we were guaranteed to have AC. On *Tanglefoot!* Mitch was blessed with such amenities. Although he about froze me out our first night on the boat before we left Ft. Myers, I now *wanted* to freeze. I welcomed it. I would have savored every shiver. We all huddled up in the cool boat, changed *again* and hung our now-sweaty post-shower clothes on doors and towel racks to dry. Claiming he needed "additional conditioning," Mitch sat right in front of the AC vent by the nav station, letting the cool air blow on his face like a dog hanging out a window.

"I'm bigger," he said into the breeze, with a bit of a *"Luke I am your father"* voice. "There's more of me to cool," he rationalized.

But Mitch did eventually find a fan in the nav area and set it up right in front of the vent so it could blow at each of us intermittently. He was like a human oscillating fan. Granted he oscillated toward himself mostly but he did blow the occasional draft our way. It was the first time since 7:00 that morning we hadn't been sweaty, and it did feel amazing. But it was only around 5:00 p.m. and the crew was absolutely beat. Mitch was sure we'd sleep "Just fine, I swear!" if we ate a 5:00 p.m. dinner, senior citizen style, and went to bed by six. Maybe the bedazzled, Aqua Net marvel we met at Marko's Diner back in Ft. Myers knew Mitch better than we did because he was certainly on the hunt for the senior citizen's special. But Phillip and I weren't so inclined, so we encouraged Mitch to hold out just a little longer while we sipped a glass of wine and relaxed on the boat.

It was also the first time since we'd stepped aboard the Nonsuch in Ft. Myers that we were just "hanging out" on Mitch's new boat—not checking the fluids, unpacking, cleaning or underway. We were just sitting down below, enjoying her and it dawned on me how really incredible Mitch's Nonsuch was. It was shockingly comfortable below, spacious, well laid out, with plenty of storage, seating and amenities like AC, a fridge, a great saloon area. A family of four could easily, and comfortably, cuddle up in there and watch a movie. I was really impressed by then with the live-aboard feel of the Nonsuch.

And I was certainly feeling it. Curled up myself on the settee on the starboard side, trying to tap out some notes from the passage, sipping wine, finally feeling clean and comfortable, and my lids started to droop. Two-hour nights shifts can be exhausting, particularly after the first night because your body has not yet had a chance to adjust. After the second night of two hours on, two hours off, I usually feel like I've acclimated a bit and I'm not nearly as tired on the third day. But that second *day*, which is where we were, is always a killer. We were trying to stay awake because we knew a "nap" would turn into a near-coma and a quest for dinner would be then out of the question.

Phillip and I wanted to at least stay up long enough to go exploring for dinner—that's half the fun of traveling—and then *really* get a good night's rest that evening so we could sail out of Clearwater fresh at first light. The goal was to make the 175 nautical-mile, thirty-six- to forty-eight-hour run to Apalachicola on our next passage or—if things were going really well (and I mean *really* well)—knock out the entire 285 nautical mile run from Clearwater all the way back to Pensacola in one shot. That would be a three- to five-day passage, if we accomplished it, and the longest Phillip and I would have been able to claim at the time.

Either way, we knew this was the "real jaunt." The passage from Ft. Myers to Clearwater had been pretty much parallel to the shore and Apalachicola over to Pensacola would also be, pretty much, a hug of the shore. This passage, however—from Clearwater to Apalachicola—would be the true Gulf crossing. This is where we would find ourselves on our longest leg of the trip and the furthest from shore. Let's just say if Mother Nature sensed any opportune time to jack us around, this would be it. And, this is the exact time, *last time*—when Phillip, Mitch and I were bringing the Niagara back from Punta Gorda, Florida to Pensacola—that she decided to really see what we were made of. The last time the three of us made this passage we found ourselves in the middle of the night, in the middle of the Gulf, sawing our dinghy off the davits in four- to six-foot seas that had sheared every bolt we had left to hold her. If there was any part of this trip to really be concerned about, this was it.

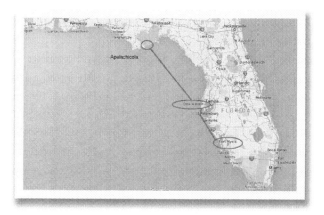

As we sat in the saloon of the Nonsuch we checked the weather, for the forty-fourth time that day. Regarding the winds: "Variable and light," they said. *"Ooh, that's new. Not,"* said the crew. It seemed like that was always the forecast during that trip. It was either that or summer squalls—typical for that time of year in Florida. Kind of annoying. It might mean more boring motoring, if that prediction held. But the sea-state looked to be calm. It definitely appeared to be a good window. We deemed it safe to go and decided we would leave the next morning as soon as we woke.

"We better get that dinner then!" Phillip said as we watched Mitch nodding off by the nav station, somehow miraculously still balancing the fan upright in his light slumber.

"Time for an adventure dinner!" I shouted, startling him up.

"Sorry," Mitch said, although I wasn't sure what for. He was tired. Phillip and I were pretty tired too. Maybe it was more knee-jerk than anything, but a part of me thought maybe he was still feeling like he had dragged Phillip along, against our will, on this tiring, torturous journey bringing his boat home. Still slugging his way through stage five I could see.

"Come on old timer!" Phillip shouted, perking him up. "Let's go!"

The last time the three of us had stopped in Clearwater we were awe-struck at the circus we stumbled into. It reminded me a lot of Mallory Square in Key West, after Phillip and I traveled there the following year. Seriously, I had been almost accosted by a man on stilts in Clearwater, mesmerized by another who played better "drums" on tipped-over five-gallon buckets than any musician I had ever seen and I had watched as a woman got a Lisa-Frank-style-kitten tattooed on the upper part of her ass. It was wild. There were also hundreds of street vendors out with pop-up card tables covered in their hand-made wares—all those kinds of useless trinkets you see in big SOUVENIER shops off the interstate like your name on a grain of rice in a magnified tube, little blown-glass creatures, rabbit's foots, your name burned into a leather bracelet and oh (*oh!*) your name (as it seems tourists need to be often reminded of their name) on a miniature Florida license plate key-chain. Good stuff.

While Phillip and I would have loved to amble along that crazy circus strip again for a couple of hours, the crew was pretty beat and Mitch groaned and moaned the entire time we did it last time, so Phillip and I decided to let him off the hook and head straight to dinner. We did want to venture to a new eatery this time, though, to try something new. The last time we had been sucked in by false advertising when the "Marina Diner" sign sported a sexy sailor gal with monstrous tits yet we were greeted by a server who looked like a pile of toothpicks glued together. This time we decided to give the long-standing Frenchy's Saltwater Cafe a try for dinner and even opted for their early bird special, without shame. Seriously, it was still only 6:00 p.m.

I could tell I was tired, though, when the only thing I felt after two stout rum drinks was sleepy. Exhaustion is a total buzzkill. It was a bit of a mumble-and-chew show at our table and I'm pretty sure Mitch fell asleep at one point, his head laid back on the wall. But I can't promise I didn't nod off at one point either. After dinner, the three of us ambled back to the boat to slumber in our frozen palace and get a solid night's rest before shoving back out into the Gulf the next day.

I don't recall setting the alarm—the Captain is extremely reliable in that regard—but I do recall it blaring out at us the next morning. Twice.

"Mitch," I said shaking his shoulder a bit. Phillip and I had already snoozed through the alarm twice before finally rolling out of bed. Mitch hadn't yet moved. After his first night holding solo shifts on an offshore passage, I'm sure that was the most tired he can remember feeling. And, I'll be nice and say that's a testament to his state of exhaustion not his memory.

"Mitch!" I shouted giving him a solid shove. He finally flinched with a snort and looked at me in total shock, as if he didn't know where he was, who I was and why the hell I was shoving him awake. I stood there with a raised eyebrow for a minute and he finally checked back into reality and started rustling out of bed. He said he couldn't even remember laying down the night before. We had all just about felt that way. But after a good ten hours of sleep we were all feeling pretty rested and ready to get underway.

We began readying the Nonsuch for passage and started talking about a plan to de-dock. Again, we had Mitch make all the decisions and simply tell us what lines to release when, and I gave him a solid A on the plan but a B on the execution. As soon as he put the boat in reverse and started to throttle her up, instantly the stern started kicked over to port. Sharp too. I was on the port side and pushing with all of my might near the beam but her stern continued to pivot around.

I looked over at Phillip on starboard but he'd already let off the bow line per Mitch's instruction and didn't have any way to control the nose of the boat. The further she kept turning, I watched with clenched teeth as the finger dock we had been using to get on and off the boat on the port side began to jut in through the lifelines. I scrambled toward it, braced my back against the cabin top and tried to push it out with my feet.

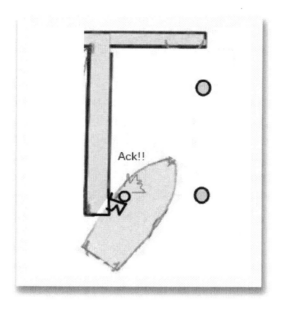

It was inching out but not fast enough. As the boat continued to move backward, the finger pier made contact with a stanchion post and I was afraid she was going to snap it over like a weed, ripping a hole in the deck in the process. *I hate docking.* Have I said that before? And de-docking too. Almost as much. It's always so stressful to watch your precious boat inch closer and closer to sure peril.

"Go forward, Mitch!" Phillip shouted. "Come back in! The same way!"

I was wedged on the deck, my feet pressing hard against the finger dock and my back against the cabin wall, trying like hell to get the finger pier out from the lifelines. I looked back at Mitch as he threw the boat in forward. His face seemed to beg me for forgiveness. I could tell he felt terrible for putting us in this position, particularly seeing me, wedged against the boat, my feet pushing on the piling.

But Mitch gassed her up, started steering her right back into the slip—along the exact haphazard path which she had come out—and he saved us! I was so glad to see the finger pier finally ease out from the lifelines and back away from the boat.

"I'm sorry, Philly, I just … I don't know," Mitch started in as Phillip and I re-secured the boat. And that's when I had it.

"Oh stop with this sorry crap!" I scolded him. "You're learning. Everybody has to. We want to help. Make the important mistakes while we're here so we *can* and *stop saying sorry*."

Mitch kind of stared at me blankly and I realized I had kind of snapped. I knew he was just trying to be nice, trying—in his way—to thank us for what we were doing for him, but I also knew the emotions he was experiencing and why he needed to forget it and move on.

I told so many people, "I'm sorry, I can't," when Phillip and I had just got our own boat. Those who don't own a boat or don't understand the cruising lifestyle often just don't get it. Often, when friends or loved ones would invite us out for dinners, birthday get-togethers, trips on the weekends, cousin Andy's graduation, Karen's baby shower, whatever, Phillip and I would have to beg off because we were either going out on the boat or going to be working on the boat. For a while, "sorry," was always my initial response. I felt guilty for having to decline and for missing some of these things. *Not the baby shower, though! The last one I went to they did that "guess the flavor of the poo" game with melted candy bars in diapers and I swore: "Never again!"*

But once I realized what I was apologizing for—doing something I loved, spending time on my boat—my guilt started to wane and my responses began less with "I'm sorry," and more often with an excited: "We'll be out on the hook that weekend!" I was sure Mitch would soon realize the same. He now had a boat and this was going to be part of his lifestyle—folks coming aboard and along for passages if they wanted to spend time with him or understanding if he chose to decline certain invitations because he would rather be on the boat. Besides, Phillip and I were making the voyage with him on the Nonsuch because we wanted to help him, but also because it's what we loved to do! While it was a lot of work, we were still grateful for the invite and probably felt like thanking him more than the other way around. *Don't tell Mitch that, though.*

"Okay," Mitch said, seeming to come around to my "no apologies" policy. "But I was *not* turning the wheel!" he said adamantly.

As I have readily admitted, I do not consider myself an experienced helmsman, but when Mitch said that, it dawned on me what likely occurred, because I had done it before—backed out cockeyed precisely *by* not turning the wheel.

"I'm sure you didn't," Phillip said, making his way back to the cockpit. I watched as he looked at the wheel, leaned over and looked at the rudder, popped back up and asked Mitch, "Where's your center?"

"I, ummm, well I ..." Mitch stuttered, looking confused for a minute before it clicked. "Oh yeah, that," he said apologetically. Phillip just nodded. He'd told Mitch to do it. Mitch knew to do it, but it wasn't a matter of knowing, but rather *remembering* to do it—checking to make sure your rudder is centered before backing out. It was an easy mistake to make that could have cost him thousands in damage. I don't man the helm often and I've made that mistake several times already. It's part of Phillip's mental checklist because he backs us out most of the time. For him, it would be a no-brainer but that's where experience comes in. *Sailing. No one said it was easy.*

Phillip just slapped Mitch on the shoulder, said "Center your wheel," and started to make his way back up topside so we could attempt that fiasco again, but I could see Mitch's hands were shaking a little and he stopped Phillip with the question that had probably been burning inside of him since he bought the boat.

"Phil, do you think I can handle this boat?" Mitch asked and my ears perked up. I did feel for him. After a scary experience like that, you start to doubt yourself.

"Of course," Phillip immediately responded, which may have sounded like placating Mitch but he wouldn't. It was the truth. He could. Like any new boat owner, Mitch just needed to make the important mistakes while help was around. With the simple fix of lining up the rudder before backing out, Mitch handled the second attempt flawlessly, even while being shaken up from the heart-pumping first attempt. I would have congratulated him but he didn't even relish in the moment. He was all business. The minute he eased her out, Mitch clocked her around, put her in forward and started heading toward the channel.

Phillip and I watched him silently for a minute like proud parents. He was doing it all by himself. A little too fast, mind you. That man cannot—for the life of him—ease off the throttle. But he was doing it.

But as soon as we were all smiles and cheering for him, his "Mitch" started showing. He was watching the GPS trying to steer his way out of the channel and he kept weaving back and forth in the narrow channel, inexplicably. Phillip and I let it slide a time or two but after a few back-and-forths we had to ask. "What's going on buddy?" I hollered from the deck. Mitch was quiet at first. Then he started muttering a little and finally said, "Oh, now I get it. I'm the long line." Phillip and I exchanged a raised-eyebrow. "You're what?" I asked. "The long line," Mitch repeated. "I couldn't tell on the GPS which line was the heading or me. But, I get it now. I'm the long line."

He was like a dog chasing his tail back there. Mitch didn't seem to have any more guilt for bringing Phillip and I along for this maiden voyage—what with us elbowing each other and giggling like two boys at a peep show over his "creative navigation"—as he got us back on course. But, our snickering aside, it seemed nothing could dampen his spirit.

"Oh, I don't care," Mitch said to no one off the starboard stern when he saw Phillip and me hiding our faces and biting back smiles. Mitch held this dopey smile out into the blue for quite some time. It was the quietest he had been the entire voyage. If I had to guess, I'll bet it was his favorite memory from the trip. He looked as happy as I can ever recall seeing him. His hand held firmly on the wheel, a bright, perky expression. Even his posture was good. So overcome with Nonsuch joy—I can only assume—he just busted out with it.

"Nonsuches never foul," Mitch said in this rich, buttery infomercial voice.

DELIRIUM

The Rare Delusion that Your Boat Can Never Foul!

Occasionally, with particularly unique affecteds, an additional stage is experienced at this time wherein the affected begins to entertain wild delusions about the subject of his grief, finding it incapable of any shortcomings of faults.

"It will work," I said, trying to convince Phillip. "Trust me," although I could tell from his skeptical face that he did not and rightfully so. *Why?* Because I was delirious.

I have to say it was jolly good fun watching our buddy Mitch graduate through each phase of boat-buying grief and step unknowingly onto the next platform, blinking into the stage lights, wondering what fresh new agony awaited him there. The next stage Mitch progressed into I personally did not anticipate. I had to think back incredibly hard on my own boat-buying emotional journey and wonder whether I had experienced this particular one. The minute it came to me, though, I knew. I had indeed been there. Except I was beyond delirious. I was delusional.

"Watch," I said, still trying to win Phillip over. "I'll just stick these two together, tie it on here with 550 cord and you pull this hook to open it."

"We're not gluing that," Phillip said, vetoing my latest in a series of redneck jerry-rigs.

When Phillip and I first brought our Niagara back home to Pensacola, and I finally got to start in on all of the little "Annie fixes" I had been dreaming up during our own passage across the Gulf, I was convinced I could create any necessary handy boat accessory wholly out of staples, Velcro, duct tape or hot glue. While some of my jerry-rigs— to Phillip's embarrassment—lasted, many proved ill-gotten ideas from the beginning. My thirty-five-foot-long power cord cover made entirely from stapled green fleece, for example, did not make the cut. The elastic band I hot-glued to make the trash can come out when you opened the hatch, Martha-Stewart-style, did not last. And when I pulled out duct tape to use as chafe guard where the genny brushes across the bow pulpit, Phillip stopped me cold. "We're not taping that," he said.

Why was he opposed? Because I had lost my marbles. I truly believed, as long as we had those four items aboard, the boat and I could handle anything. *Who needs spare impellers, fuel filters or zincs? Please. That's child's play.* Now it seemed Mitch had succumb to the same delirium with this "Nonsuches never foul" bit.

Phillip and I both turned to look at him, thinking he had truly done it. Gone mad.

"They may make slight indiscretions," Mitch continued, with this little finger wagging *tssk-tssk* action now looking at Phillip and me both in earnest. "But they *never* foul."

It had to have been true. Mitch didn't care what we thought of him then, because he truly seemed bonkers. Not only was he talking to himself, he was doing so in a cheesy gameshow host fashion and he wasn't even making any sense. I think Phillip and I remained silent just for the pure entertainment factor. If Mitch had really blown a fuse, we wanted to see where this crazy train was headed.

Friends, I must say, on that stagnant day in the Gulf, our lively buddy Mitch regaled us. I mentioned all of the boat porn he had trolled through before settling on the Nonsuch but I had not realized—until this passage—the degree to which Mitch had delved, reaching deep in the Nonsuch archives to find these locked-away Nonsuch promotional videos from the seventies on YouTube.

"They've got this lady at the helm, see," Mitch started in. "And she's wearing a full-length white linen skirt. All the way down, dusting the docks as she breezes by everybody on her way to her Nonsuch."

Mitch, as best he could, was putting on a dainty little rendition of Ms. Breezy as she flitted by all the drooling sailors at the docks.

"And, when she gets to her Nonsuch, *s/v Rainbow*," Mitch says with flare and I watched the whites of Phillip's eyes bulge out. I didn't want to laugh because the story was getting *so good* and I didn't want to break Mitch's focus. "She steps on board, unties one line with her forefinger and thumb," Mitch re-enacted it, with a proper pinkie out, "and she's off, *'Turning on a dime!'* the ad says."

My head was buried in my hands at this point. I was shaking it, peeking up at Mitch between fingers, begging him to continue. And he did. *Oh my God he did.* Mitch regaled us for an hour at least with dozens of different scenes from these seventies ads—the Nonsuch tacking with ease, the Nonsuch in a heated race, a friendly mimosa-laden brunch, hosted on the Nonsuch.

And while Mitch's re-enactment will remain forever burned in my memory, it wasn't until months later when I was struck by the desire to find the ancient videos and watch them for myself that I realized the one thing Mitch failed to mention about them was their distinct soft-core seventies-porn feel.

Maybe Mitch did not want to talk about this particular aspect of the videos in front of me. *I doubt it.* Or perhaps he—as someone actually *in* the market for a Nonsuch—was so captivated by them, so ensnared that he didn't even notice they were using the one thing that always sells: sex. I kid you not. Without Mitch even noticing, every line of the video sounded like Joey Tribbiani's dirty version of "grandma's chicken salad." Let your dirty mind run free with these:

Looks like a cat, moves like a leopard.

She makes you feel at home just thinking about her.

Everything is easy. It's like she's anxious to get underway.

When Nonsuch meets Nonsuch a kind of happy magic happens.

"So," he says, "are you going to the regatta?"
"You bet," she replies.
"Want to go together?" she asks.
"Sure. My Nonsuch or yours?"
"Mine, but I'll race you home for privilege."
(*What does that even mean? Whose privilege?*)

Like a dolphin ballet. (*Because we all know what dolphins do best, right?*)

Just as much fun to do as to see. (*Translation: You can watch, that's okay.*)

There's a kind of silent bugle blowing when Nonsuches come together.

It's the call of the wind and the sea, and just a hint of champagne.

Come on in Nonsuch, there's always room for one more.

When Nonsuches race, they race in a civilized manner. It is very unsuch to protest.

While Nonsuches might occasionally commit slight indiscretions, they never (*ever!*) foul.

And our favorite: "We also call her Nonsuch because there isn't anything like her or the people who sail her."

Good stuff, right? The three of us spent a good bit of that bright blue day repeating the Nonsuch mantras back and forth as we continued our way across the Gulf. It's amazing what you find the time to talk about, re-enact and share out there when it's hours upon hours, spent mostly all together in the cockpit. There's no internet. No cell signal. No T.V. Not even YouTube. You talk, you read, you write. And you get real creative out there.

I had been working away on the laptop for most of the trip, which irritated Mitch a bit because when he's talking, he likes you to look at him. Do you have any friends like that? *Their stories are engaging. Riveting actually. They deserve eye contact. You got that?* I know it irked Mitch a little when my eyes would drift back to my screen and he could hear the keystrokes while he was telling us some story he'd likely already told us two-and-a-half times. Finally he could take it no more.

"What are you ratta-tatting over there?" he asked, when I hadn't offered a *"Really? Then what?"* to his last cliffhanger.

"My next book," I said.

"Is this one all about *me* again?" he asked, all huffy, referring to my write-up of this hapless crew's first salty passage together.

"No," I replied flatly and fought the urge to wrestle with him over the all-about-him remark.

"Oh," he said, now seeming a little deflated. *That man. If the story is Gilligan's Island, you either want to be the goofy star or you don't.*

"In fact, you're not even in it," I said, a little smile starting to curl. *I loved teasing him.* But, he did push me to do something that day that was incredibly fun, engaging, challenging for me and that entertained the entire crew for at least the same amount of time that Mitch's Nonsuch seventies ads did. He asked me to tell him the story, as detailed as I wanted to be. *I mean, we had plenty of time.* And he promised to listen all the way through before critiquing, which was a generous offer. For Mitch.

I was a little nervous because I had not yet even pitched this particular book idea to Phillip. I always wait to pitch to him because he is my toughest and most honest critic—which makes him my most valuable. I always like to have everything wired tight before I bring it to Phillip, so to speak. But, I was getting close to that point, or so I believed.

And here we were. Ambling our way across the blue with nothing better to do. And Mitch had asked. So off I went, telling the tale. It was *Keys to the Kingdom*. A rough draft mind you, but it was the beginnings of *my* story, the tale of my transition from an overworked, stress-frazzled lawyer to a broke bachelorette who now owned significantly less but had the refreshing new freedom to live more.

The boys were quiet, listening intently, nodding here and there as I laid it all out, asking no questions but giving a few "*hmm*" and "*aha*" faces at a couple of key places. I was expecting a kind of rigorous cross-examination afterward, particularly from Mitch who had—true to his word—remained quiet the entire time. He had only one question.

"So, is there like a lot of sailing in it?" Mitch asked.

Everything I just told you and that's your one question? "Yesss," I hissed. "Like I said, it's like *Salt of a Sailor*, in that it covers a particular passage on the boat but it will also have flashbacks to stories from my past, except this book will cover mine and Phillip's trip to the Keys last year. *Keys to the Kingdom*, get it?"

"Okay, but not *too many* old stories, right?" Mitch asked. "You're not even that old."

I wasn't quite sure what that even meant. Not old enough to have 'old' stories or not old enough to be allowed to tell them if I did? I turned to Phillip hoping for, I wasn't sure what. Support? Back-up?

"Let me digest it," was all he said.

I won't say I was defeated but I was frustrated. It wasn't disapproval by any means but it was not a reassuring reception. But this is always the case when you decide to write, to create, to put something out there for the masses to devour. They may welcome you into their approving arms or they may gnash and nip at you with their sharp teeth. I find it's usually some mix of both, no matter what you create.

Alright more sailing. Less old/ not-yet-old stories, I told myself as I huffed my way to the bow to curl up with my laptop and write some more. What can I say? I love a challenge. Writing is the ultimate one. I wrote the majority of that book from the bow of Mitch's Nonsuch, staring out at a calm blue horizon.

But I did have to let myself, at times, put away the clicking gizmo and just sit, look out on the silky water before me—sometimes for a half hour, sometimes almost two—and realize what an awesome opportunity this was and what an incredible adventure I was on. Here Phillip and I were, back again in an embankment of blue. We were still young and capable and in control of our careers enough that we could steal away for an offshore cruise like this and embark on many of our own in the coming years. I was finally living the life I wanted to live and it felt incredible! The view from my "new office" was fantastic and it was always changing! All I needed was a lap, a top for it and occasional internet, and my only concern was what I was going to eat for dinner and whether I wrote a good book.

Oh, and the motor. I was concerned about the motor.

With wind that wouldn't disturb a dandelion, she was currently the only thing chugging us across that body of blue. Phillip had noticed a spot of pink on the oil pad underneath the engine around noon. I call that little absorbent wonder the "engine diaper" because it literally catches all of the engine's crap. It's also handy because it keeps those nasty fluids from making their way down to nasty up the bilge and it helps you keep an eye on what almighty important fluids are dripping out of your engine. We could not recall, however, if the pink spot was there when we first started out back in Ft. Myers two days ago or if it was in fact a new spot, that had just formed while we were now pushing out of Clearwater on our way to Apalachicola. For that reason, Phillip left the engine access open while we motored that afternoon to keep an eye on it.

After a few hours of motoring, it was clear the drop was new. I almost couldn't believe it. The parallels were a little too uncanny. Here we were, the three of us, traveling once again across the Gulf together in another 1985 boat Hinterhoeller-built boat, and we had another transmission leak. Phillip and I had just sailed our Niagara out of Apalachicola Bay—after having the transmission we had seized up solid on the first passage replaced—when we found a leak under the shifter arm, just like Mitch was facing here. I almost felt like I was staring at the same engine, counting the same drip. I wondered if Bill Murray was going to show up with that stupidly-animated groundhog and count with me.

The thought ran through my head to check and make sure we had saved some extra Dasani water bottles in case I needed to whip up another duct tape fluid-catchment contraption (patent-pending) like I had last time. Perhaps I wasn't as delirious as Phillip thought with my duct tape addiction, because it had sure saved us on the Niagara then. Such measures didn't seem necessary on Mitch's Nonsuch (yet), as we were only getting one drop of hot pink transmission fluid about once every two minutes. Not a huge amount. But it was certainly something we wanted to keep an eye on in case it increased. It was coming out from under the shifter arm—just as it had during the inaugural run of the new transmission on our boat—probably because, Phillip and I assumed, like our boat as well, the ole' Westie on the Nonsuch had not been worked that hard in a long time and the same ninety-seven cent gasket on the shifter arm was wearing out.

It felt a little odd knowing exactly what the problem was and exactly how to fix it just by looking at it. Such are the benefits of experience. It was a little wild to see the very same thing happening to Mitch that had happened to us, but I imagine the more you cruise the more you start to see it all. Imagine all of the breakdowns and jerry-rigs Kretschmer has seen. Orange fluid starts to pour out of the faucet in the head and he'd say: "Oh, that's nothing, just some compensating fluid for your alternator. A slight overflow. I can fix it with a toothpick."

It seemed that answer made about as much sense as our shifter-arm-gasket diagnosis did to Mitch. He sat there, Indian style, in front of the engine swapping confused looks between Phillip, then me, then the shifter arm on the transmission.

"What about when we shift? Will it just start pouring out? Should we not shift anymore?" he asked.

I had to look away to hide my smile. *No Mitch, we shouldn't. We should keep her in forward all the way home!* Granted, I knew he was just spouting off questions out of concern and I was sure he just meant keep her in gear until we turned the motor off. Pretty sure at least. But it was still kind of cute to see him, this big tall man, curled up and hunched over, staring at his poor little engine with such worry. When Phillip and I were doing the same after our engine broke down in Carrabelle, Florida, Mitch was out looking for curly fries. The thought ran through my mind to ask Mitch right then if he had a hankering for curly fries. *I'm evil.* But I didn't, so apparently I'm not. Entirely.

"It'll be fine," Phillip finally soothed him. "Shifting won't have an impact on it, but we need to see how much transmission fluid is in there."

I hopped up into the cockpit to shut down the engine so we could check the level and see how much pink goodness was still splashing around in the transmission. The sun was just starting to set so we decided to put together our chicken tiki masala dish for dinner while the engine was cooling.

"What is nann?" Mitch asked, pronouncing it like the "nann" in Nanny Boo Boo, when I pulled out the package of naan. He gave us such fits over it while he was checking off our provisions list for the passage, claiming no one at Publix had ever heard of it. I'm sure it didn't help him pronouncing it "nann," and telling them it was "like a tortilla." There's none such like Mitch.

He loved it, though, and we were glad to see Mitch had no queasiness this time around. He was scarfing up the masala we had made for dinner mumbling, "Nann is great," between bites.

"Where do you get this stuff?" he asked after he popped in his last fluffy bite.

"Publix," we replied.

We certainly got the best seats in the house for dinner, too. If the dropped bimini is like leaving the tent at night, during the daytime it's like stepping out of the house onto the sun-soaked veranda. Suddenly your world is opened. A gentle blanket of blue lapped around us, stretching as far as we could see in every direction, glinting in the sun. We still had no wind to speak of. Even the three to four mile-an-hour gusts we were getting (*ooh!*) were coming at us right on the nose, so motoring was still going to be the only option. But, there was really no reason to complain in light of the view.

It was Phillip's turn to clean up after dinner so he started rounding up and washing the dishes while I helped Mitch check the level on the transmission fluid now that the engine had cooled.

"I can't see it," Mitch was squinting and twirling the transmission dipstick in front of his face. "There's nothing in there." Clearly Mitch

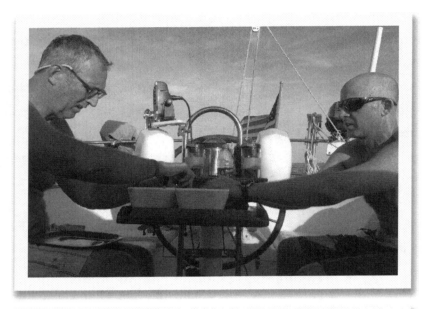

was still wading through his delirium stage. Not only do Nonsuches "Never foul!" but apparently, in Mitch's surreal world, they also run perfectly fine without transmission fluid.

"There can't be nothing," I told him. "There's a little etched-out ring at the bottom of the stick. You have to look at it right when you pull it out and it should be pink."

I agreed with him that it is sometimes hard to see, particularly if the transmission fluid is still hot. It is thinner then, more translucent, but still visible. And I could tell the stick was wet as Mitch twirled it because it was reflecting the last rays of sunlight from the cockpit. But he was holding it upside down, which did not help.

"Let me try," I said as I scooched him out of the way. I cleaned and dried the stick, bolt to tip, stuck it back in and looked immediately at the tip when I pulled it out. My head kicked back in surprise. Partly because Mitch was right—that's just rare—but mostly because he was right! There wasn't any pink in the ring. None. I could see now it was still dry. I dipped it again and found still no pink in the ring. It did leave a pink drop on my paper towel though so I knew there had to be some sliver of fluid down there. I dried and dipped again and this time saw it—a tiny little brim of pink at the very base of the tip, *well* below the ring. I dried and dipped one more time to be sure and I was sure.

"Get me some transmission fluid," I told Mitch, which peaked Phillip's interest from the galley.

"I'm glad we checked," Phillip said when I showed him the pink sliver at the bottom of the stick.

"Me too."

It was hard to believe we had darn near run another one completely out. She was thirsty, too. When Mitch came back with the bottle, the old gal downed a third of it and insisted we keep the bottle tipped up. In all, we put a half-quart of transmission fluid in and were shocked to see her take that much. I was grateful Phillip had thought to check for leaks and had spotted this one in time to stop another disaster. With every passage I undertook, I was learning, more and more, how important it is to monitor everything. Often a catastrophic and costly failure can be prevented very easily and inexpensively simply by keeping a watchful eye on the boat and her many systems.

Once we finally had a good layer of pink fluid on the ring, we cranked the engine back up and put her under load to monitor again. It was still one drip about every two minutes. A very slow drip overall, but it looked like we would be doing a good bit of motoring throughout the night. I tried to mentally calculate the minute-drip-math but it soon became clear I hadn't a clue how many "drips" are in a quart of transmission fluid. With the many uncanny similarities between our first passage across the Gulf and now Mitch's, I was almost afraid to ask him but we needed to know.

"How much transmission fluid you got on board, buddy?"

Mitch kind of kept his eyes forward, staring at the drip spot like I was, waiting another minute and forty-five seconds for the next one. He either didn't or he pretended like he didn't hear me because he didn't *want* to respond. I asked again.

"Mitch, how much transmission fluid do you have?"

"That much," he finally said, turning his eyes to the bottle still in my hand. If he thought that amount was going to get us home, he really *was* delusional.

"Apalachicola it is," I said.

CHAPTER SIX

BARGAINING:

Ineffective Attempts to Negotiate a Better Boat Fate

In a final effort to un-do the situation, the affected may try to compromise or bargain with others. For example, he may try to bargain with a higher power in exchange for impossible results.

I don't think I was angry. I'm not sure I would have thought to have brought more than a quart of transmission fluid for a trip like this where we were planning to dot along the shore, particularly when it was full when we left and we had a whole quart on board. Generally, that's enough transmission fluid for a passage like this. I guess the only reason I would bring more would be purely as a result of what happened to Phillip and me on our first passage and that's kind of a silly reason. Lightning shouldn't strike in the same place twice, right? *Right?!*

If you're the only stick on the horizon it will. It was surprising to find ourselves in the same predicament, but Phillip and I believed the remaining half-quart would at least get us the rest of the way across the Gulf to Apalachicola, assuming we had to motor the whole way. If we got wind, we would be in really good shape. Surely there would be a chance we would do *some* sailing on this trip. *Just some!* I think somewhere deep inside Phillip and I were nurturing a tiny hope that we would run out of fluids so that we would *have to* sail. Don't tell Mitch.

Mitch, however, wasn't thinking that at all.

"Just … hang in there," I heard him say although it was more of a mumble. I almost knee-jerked a *"What?"* in response but I'm glad I didn't because Mitch wasn't talking to me and—once I realized he wasn't—I wanted to see who he was pleading with down there. He was hunkered over the engine, pouring some of that precious pink nectar back in and he was talking to her. The transmission.

"Not much longer now," he whispered to her. Mitch's delirium was obviously gone and, once reality began setting in—that his boat *could* foul without fluids—he quickly graduated to the next phase of his grieving process. Cue stage six: bargaining. Mitch was down there, talking to the transmission, trying to negotiate a settlement. I'm sure he promised her quarts, even gallons, of fresh pink goop as long as she would keep running. Whatever he offered, it must have worked, because she turned over like a champ and began chugging along. I told you, he is quite the salesman. Obviously a better one than me because I recalled my own bargaining with our boat had not gone so well.

"Is it not supposed to drip?" I remembered asking Phillip when we were cruising our boat back from Key West the year prior and discovered the stuffing box on the transmission was dripping raw water into the bilge. I honestly didn't know. Some systems on the boat, the engine for example, need to pull in water as coolant then spit it back out. I had no clue what a "stuffing box" even did, much less if it got hot and would then need coolant, but I was hoping against the odds that the drip we had discovered was a totally normal one. *I believe my delirium was just fading at the time.*

"It's called a dripless, so … no," Phillip said bluntly. "Stay down below and monitor the drip when I put her under load," Phillip said as he left me hunkered down in front of the exposed engine on our Niagara while he made his way back to the helm. And there I sat, much like Mitch, pleading with a higher transmission power that the drip would stop entirely. Apparently I didn't promise enough pink goop because it did not. The drip continued, once every ten-or-so seconds, when Phillip throttled her up. It was scary to think any minute the box could somehow shift or blow and allow the drip to become a full-fledged flow and sink the boat. Considering it in that light, a drip seemed the lesser of two evils, so I changed bargaining tactics.

"Please just drip," I kept telling her. "Just. Drip."

And so she did, all the way home to Pensacola where we then had to haul her out of the water to replace the stuffing box. Boats are such fun! I recalled we flirted with the idea then of re-rigging the boat as our original 1985 rod rigging was over thirty years old at the time.

"Is that bad?" I had asked Phillip. Knowing nothing about rigging back then, I thought, perhaps, it might strengthen over time like petrified wood. *Maybe forty-year old rigging is even better!* Phillip assured me it was not and that one of the problems with rod rigging is that it does not show signs that it is about to fail. It works great until it explodes. But, we knew a re-rig was going to be an extensive and costly project, though, so we planned to put it off at that time and wait until we were planning a big offshore voyage, so I began my bargaining again. "Hang in there ladies," I whispered to our rods. "We'll take care of you soon."

Now here was Mitch, doing the same. "Hang in there gal," I heard him say to Westie.

Phillip throttled up a bit more to—I'm going to say—help with our progress toward Apalachicola not burn through the transmission fluid, but they were undeniably one and the same. Once we were chugging back along at five knots, talk turned to the divvying up of our night shifts. The group collectively decided the two-hour shift formula we followed last time spanned too early into the evening and too late into the morning. None of us were really ready to hit the sack by 8:00 p.m. and none of us were sleeping in until 8:00 a.m. either. In addition, a shorter night-watch time-span to divvy up would mean shorter shifts for each crew member, which is always preferred. We settled on one and a half-hour shifts beginning at 9:30 p.m. and rotating until 6:30 a.m.

We also knew Phillip deserved a better deal this time because he'd taken on two true, no-one-else-is-up-with-you night shifts the last time. This meant either Mitch or I were going to have to take on the two-night-shift regime. Mitch called it before I could even put pen to paper by playing the age card.

Yes *Mitch* played that card, not us. He played it often. "You guys have to remember I'm an old guy," he would say as he handed me a screwdriver and sent me down into a cubby, or picked up some pillows leaving Phillip to lug two bags of ice. The funny thing is, though. He's not. Not at all in my opinion. I can't remember the exact number. He's like fifty-eight years young or something like that. But the man still gets out and kitesurfs for crying out loud. He paddles. He sails. He rides a Harley. *Or whatever kind of bike. It's like Coke, they're all Harleys to me.* And he was now a bonafide boat owner and sailor. He's easily one of the

coolest fifty-eight-year-olds I know, but apparently—for the record—when it comes to night shifts, he's old.

While my lawyer self was sure his particular use of the age card here was some form of reverse age discrimination, I let it go. Night sailing can really be an incredible experience and Phillip and I had agreed to make this trip with Mitch for two reasons. First, to help him get his new boat home safe. *Okay, sure that's important.* But, Phillip and I also wanted to get some more offshore experience under our belt and enjoy another invigorating Gulf-crossing while doing it. In short, we wanted an adventure! Night sailing certainly falls in that category so I told myself Mitch's loss was my gain and it was decided.

New Night Shifts

9:30 – 11 Mitch

11 – 12:30 Annie

12:30 – 2 Phillip

2 – 3:30 Mitch

3:30 – 5 Annie

5 – 6:30 Phillip

The sunset that evening was a surprise—stunning in a new way. Sometimes the sun becomes this fiery little pink ball—so bright you can barely look at it—and it paints the sky with vibrant purples and

reds before it drops down. But it didn't that night. One of the most beautiful things about the sunset is that each one is different. The saying "You've seen one, you've seen them all," could never apply. This one was breathtaking in a different way. The sun lit the sky with smooth yellows and creams. It was like we were traveling in one of those sepia-toned photographs. Everything had a vintage, weathered-around-the-corners look. I went up to the bow to soak it in and watch the sun melt like butter into the sea.

Some may find it frightening to not see shore, to not—without the assistance of charts, a compass or a GPS—know which way will lead you back home. Some fear this detachment. Phillip and I love it. He came up and sat next to me at the bow and we both relished in the moment. It felt so good to be back out in the Gulf. It was strange to think it was the same body of water that had rocked and tossed us last time, submerged and swallowed our dinghy, because it now looked so calm. It was hard to believe it was the same body of water. She had seemed so angry last time. I knew it was not personal, but I had to wonder why she had been so vicious before and now so serene. What was the reason behind it? If any?

Whatever the method to her madness, she had decided this time to dole us out conditions so smooth sailing became impossible. There wasn't even enough wind to push us. No waves to rock us. While it was definitely beautiful—still blue water in every direction—I hated to say it, but part of me wished for some small swells. *Just small ones!* Or perhaps just a nice breeze to run downwind on—something, at least to allow us to feel the boat swim beneath us and break up the monotony of our motoring.

Have you ever done that, though? Wished for the slightest bit of adventure and Mother Nature knocks you flat like a toothpick in front of a fog horn. She doesn't really do "slight." At least she doesn't for me, and I was sure she wouldn't on this trip. The minute I just cupped that little seed-of-a-thought in my hand, not yet even thinking of planting it, she reared her gnarly head at us and started brewing up big, billowing thunderheads on our stern. Phillip looked over at me immediately at the sound of the first deep rumble. I honestly felt so guilty I almost did what I normally do when I cause something but don't want to admit it: throw my hands and shoulders in the air and swear up and down, "It wasn't me!"

But it was. It was totally me. I had gotten sick of motoring and let my little sick thoughts get the best of me.

I tried not to make eye contact with the boys as the clouds closed in, fearing they might sense my culpability. I didn't want a big storm to crash on us, but I'll admit to a little tinge of excitement each time we heard a muffled rumble. That feeling changed, however, when we watched as a shocking white crack of lightning speared out and traveled the sky. There was no denying it now. But there was no point in saying it aloud either. It was clear. We had a massive thunderstorm on our stern, chasing us across the Gulf.

We watched for an hour as spindly white bolts continued to break through and shoot out in five different directions. It was beautiful but still a little frightening and also thrilling. It is unbelievable how fast lightning can travel. Three miles, maybe more, in an instant. The lightning show was mesmerizing and, thankfully, that's all it turned out to be—a show. Big, rumbling lightning storms seemed to brew up just about every day on that trip.

Once we were sure the storm was going to stay at bay, we decided to keep the bimini down for the night and I actually found myself, as I tucked in for my first rest shift, excited to wake up in a couple of hours and hold my first night shift under the stars! With two fifty-watt and a hundred-watt solar panel now mounted firmly on ours, sailing unfettered under a canvas of stars is not something Phillip and I were going to experience any time soon on our Niagara. Not intentionally, anyway. Plus, the bimini on Mitch's boat is huge! It has to be. The cockpit is huge. It's like holding an umbrella over an elephant. You're going to need a big one. I'm pretty sure the soft-core videos ring true. No matter how many you've got in there, "there's always room for one more." So, dropping it really makes a drastic difference. There was no tent anymore. Now we were just laying on sleeping bags under the stars.

With the bimini down, the motor chugging along and the autopilot doing all the work the only real job I had during my shift was to monitor the instruments and the horizon. Sometimes it is that easy. Sometimes. You pay for those times, however, when it's not at all easy, when you're man-handling a weather-heavy helm in twenty-knot winds, crashing through waves, listening for things that might break, snap, pop, tear. Some nights are like that, which is why I had no guilt in savoring the night that I was having.

The coaming around the cockpit in the Nonsuch has this wide, fat strip of teak on it that feels like it was meant to touch the soles of bare feet. Even tethered in, I could step up on it, holding onto the sail for support and walk (or dance) along it with an unfettered 360-degree view of our horizon. Yes, I said dance. There is often dancing involved in my night shifts. I usually pop a headphone in one ear for some tunes and leave the other tuned to the boat and sails, and I found the perfect accompaniment to my starlit stage that night: Lorde's *A World Alone*.

At least I thought it was perfect, not only because of the hypnotic beat but she even mentioned sailing! At least I thought she did. I am notorious for belting out the wrong lyrics to songs. Yet I belt anyway. I sing what I *think* I hear which is often not at all what the artist intended. It's like the "pour some shook-up ramen" syndrome. What did I think Toto said in their famous "Hold the Line" song? Golden Eye! I did. For years. And I belted/sang it that way every time I heard the song until Phillip finally heard *me* one day and totally called me out. Rightfully so.

On Lorde's song, I thought she said "Raise a glass cause I'm not done sailing." So that's what I sang each time I let it play during my shift that night. And if you're thinking: *That's strange. Why would Lorde bust out all of a sudden with a lyric about sailing when that's not at all what the song is about?* I would have to say: *"Silly you."* You assume I know what the song is actually about. That would require the ability to hear actual lyrics—a talent I do not possess.

I liked the replacement sailing lyric so much I decided to keep it—
even after I learned the actual lyric is "saying it" not "sailing"—and I like
to listen to the song while sailing now for that very reason. I played it
approximately 16.5 times during my first shift that night, standing up on
tiptoes on the coaming, breathing in the cool night air and belting it out.
"Cause I'm not done sailing!"

The music seemed to beat in my chest, my rib cage thudding like a
drum. It was a perfect, crisp night and the lightning, while frightening,
was still beautiful. I felt like I was a little drunk. Not falling-down drunk.
Just rolling around in all the sensations around me, giddy with my own
energy. The smooth, slick teak under my feet. The night air, sticky and
cool at once. The millions upon millions of stars I could see overhead.
And the music.

Have you ever had music do that to you? Reach into your chest,
grab your ribs and roll your head back. Music that feels like it's playing
inside your body. Pulsing within you? That sounds a little orgasmic and
maybe it was. But I was saturated with pleasure. Until I replace that
memory with another more gripping one during an offshore passage
that is still, to this day, my favorite night spent sailing on a boat.

"I like it," Phillip said, startling me a little. He had woken on his
own for his 12:30 a.m. shift and was coming up a little early, smiling at
the sight of me up there, dancing on the coaming.

"Like what?" I asked.

"The book. *Keys to the Kingdom.* It needs some serious work to
smooth it all together, but you've got a great message."

I smiled back at him. Man it felt good to hear Phillip say that. There are not a lot of people in this world that I worry myself to impress, but he is one. We sat up together in the cockpit talking about the book for a bit, different sub-themes I could weave in, some effective metaphors. It was that very night—with Phillip and I both uninhibited, cruising underneath a smattering of stars—that I knew exactly what that book would be about: breaking free. *"Raise your glass cause I'm not done sailing!"*

My mind drifted into a deep, soothing sleep when I went below to rest for my next shift at 3:30 a.m. I remember feeling so content, my life so full. Like Mitch said, I wasn't even old yet and yet, here I was, free. I was sailing. I had this incredible man in my life who craved what I craved and we had a boat, the perfect boat, to do it in. The lyrics continued to play in mind as I closed my eyes on Phillip at the helm and drifted to sleep. *"You're my best friend and we're dancing in this world alone."*

Sadly my 3:30 a.m. was nowhere near that serene. I had watched, during my previous shift, a small lightning storm brew up way behind us, to the south, and I wondered what it would feel like if a bolt zipped all the way across the sky and just pricked me. Not enough to stop my heart or anything but just enough to give me a little zap. Those were the kinds of wondrous things I pondered during *that* shift. Now it looked like I might get my stupid wish.

Clouds eased in around us and the stars faded to blackness. The motor was still pumping along. I hated to see her working that hard, but with zip wind, there was no other choice. The autopilot was still holding steady so there was not much to really do other than monitor the gauges and the horizon and thankfully it did not storm on us that night. For whatever reason, I found that shift paired better with Tommy James and

The Shondells' *Crimson and Clover* and I sang that one "over and over!" to help bide the time. I even scolded myself in the moment. Here I was, on this big adventure, supposed to be savoring every minute and I was wishing time away. But I was. I was just tired at 4:00 a.m. that morning. Until your body gets used to the shift schedule, that first night on a passage—as we were from Clearwater to Apalachicola—is always tough.

I was thrilled when I heard Phillip start to putter around below around 4:45 a.m. He was always good about waking up a little before his shift to get adjusted and ready for watch. I was trying not to look too eager to hand the wheel over to him but when he came up into the cockpit and sat first on the port side lazarette, he might have seen a slight frown. I was so ready to crash back down on the settee and let sleep take me over. But I sat with him for a minute, relaying our conditions. The storm was still thick on our stern but seemed to be inclined to stay there. Everything else was purring along and we were making good way at five knots an hour towards Apalachicola with an ETA of early afternoon the next day. Phillip jotted everything down in the log book while I watched him, my fingers drumming on the wheel. When he finally eased in behind me at the helm, I could already start to feel my body shutting down system by system. My shoulders loosened, my lids drooped. Within seconds I had sunk into the settee, consciousness already slipping away.

I felt like I was a million miles away when I heard Phillip's voice. It sounded like he was trying to shout at me through a big tub of Jell-O.

"Go wake Mitch," he said again. This time it got through. My eyes were open but I felt like I couldn't see anything. I was still so groggy and my night vision hadn't yet kicked in.

"Why? What's wrong?" I asked Phillip through my haze. My sight was coming back slowly and I could see from the clock on VHF below that it was 5:30 a.m. I had only slept for thirty minutes. It had felt like hours.

"Nothing's wrong," Phillip said with a smile, almost wagging his tail behind the helm. "We've got wind!"

I can't even say I was irritated anymore by being waken not thirty minutes after I'd laid down to indulge in the sleep of the gods, because you couldn't possibly be mad at him. Phillip was so genuinely excited by the prospect of sailing, he was practically beaming, letting the wind whip right through his teeth facing into the breeze. Had it been our boat, he would have thrown out the sails without even waking me. He's done that before. I woke below to the thunderous rattling of the rigging as the sail billowed out. It sounded like the whole dang boat was falling apart and I scrambled to the cockpit only to see the Captain there, winching the genny in, smiling like a kid at a truck rally. I'm sure he thought about hoisting the sails on his own on the Nonsuch that night but I don't care what those seventies soft-core videos say, that big-ass sail does not "raise with ease."

And I hated to admit it. *Bad sailor, Annie. Bad!* But a huge part of me wanted to politely decline, just tell Phillip, "No. I don't think we should raise that big ass sail right now in the dark. Let's just keep on motoring and sleep." My sleepy self said that, internally. However, the inclination quickly passed. Once I started moving about, stepped up into the cockpit and got some crisp night air in my lungs, I knew it was a great idea. Phillip was right. The wind had kicked up. It was blowing ten, maybe twelve, right on our stern. *Perfect for the big-ass sail!* And it was certainly time to give old Westie a much-needed break. "Raise your glass," said *Tanglefoot*, "cause I'm not done sailing!"

It took an act of Congress, though, to get the slumbering beast known as Mitch up. I shook and shouted and shook some more and he rolled around a few times. But when he finally realized where he was and what was going on—"We're finally going to do some sailing on this fine vessel of yours, sir!"—he perked up.

Soon we were all three top-side getting ready to hoist the sail. I was at the mast again helping pull the halyard down to raise the sail. While I could muscle it about 75% of the way up, I was useless the last 25%. There was just nothing I could do but watch as that halyard stretched— taut as thread—and yelped out with every crank on the winch. Phillip had already told Mitch one of the first things he should do after we brought the boat back to Pensacola was have a strong track put in to make raising the main easier, but he said it again then for good measure. "You have *got* to get a strong track Mitch," as he cranked again and again on the winch, each round ending in a wicked squeal from the halyard. After two dozen painful yelps around the winch, we got it up and clocked it out to starboard to catch the wind.

The belly of the sail stretched and pulled taut when she found the wind. I have mentioned the sail is big, right? *Boy is it!* It's like hoisting a barn door up into the wind. This was our first time to sail downwind on the Nonsuch and we were truly learning how much she likes to be pushed!

"I'm gonna wake y'alls asses up to do some sailing!" Phillip hollered when we had the sail full and was finally moving along by the power of the wind. And I'm not paraphrasing there. Phillip says "y'alls." When he's excited enough. Mitch was fiddling with the choker and watching the body of the sail and while I still claim to be no expert in sailing the Nonsuch, I don't believe Mitch qualified as one yet either at that point. The choker was a completely new system to me. I guess if you wanted to analogize it, it operates much like the outhaul on our sloop. Crank her

in and she flattens the sail. Let her out and the sail bags.

This was our first time sailing downwind, so the boys were really wanting to fiddle with the sails and see what responses they could get from the boat by making tweaks here and there. They were both eyeing the sail, pulling this in, letting that out, watching everything. I was watching it too, as the choker cinched in tight near the mast, I could see the sail pull tight. I stepped around the front to see how close the choker was to the mast. My chest laid on the mast and focusing solely up on that point—where the choker pulls in near the mast—I didn't see it coming. None of us did. It's like we were all so focused on the bugs on the leaves that we couldn't see the forest was on fire. To this day I still

wonder what would have happened had I been aft of the mast.

We'd had the sail pushed far out to starboard, trying to use wind that was dead on our stern to hold a course toward Apalachicola. With the boys fiddling and fussing and focusing on the lines in the cockpit, Phillip let her ease a little too far to starboard and the sail started to flirt with the idea of shifting to center. Flirting soon turned into a sloppy make-out scene at the bar and, before I knew it, the old gal was lifting up her skirt and ready to give it up.

"Phillip!" was all I could get out before the sail on the Nonsuch thundered over and slammed to port with a sickening aluminum clang. The boat groaned over to port as the sail filled on the other side. The mast was still ringing in my hands as I shot a look back to the cockpit. Phillip was hunched over the wheel, one hand covering his head. Mitch was nowhere in sight. I almost couldn't believe we had just done that.

Accidental jibe.

On a boat with a sail the size of Kansas! I did mention the sail on the Nonsuch is big, right? Well, however big you may think it is, when it's barreling over the deck, threatening everything in its path, it's bigger than that. Plus, the wishbone boom is just as big! Roughly thirty feet, the length of the boat. The bone you'll be wishing it does *not* hit as it rakes over the cockpit is your skull.

Phillip gave a quick frantic look up to the mast to confirm I was still aboard, and I was grateful when I saw Mitch's head and shoulders clamber up from the cockpit floor. Everyone seemed to be intact but we did suffer one casualty–the outboard on the stern rail. Or, the PVC extender arm on the tiller of the outboard at least. The thing was smashed into pieces. The sail also caught the choker handle on the outboard on the way over and yanked that out too.

Mitch had a theory on it. He surmised it was Phillip's attempt to take out *his* outboard in vengeance because we'd had to sacrifice our outboard to Poseidon during our last passage with Mitch. It was just that, though. A theory. Phillip said he was just focusing on the choker and accidentally let the boat point a little too far to starboard and then BOOM. First downwind lesson learned. The accidental jibe? Not fun on any such, but particularly un-fun on the Nonsuch. They should add a little finger-wagging *tssk, tssk* warning to those Nonsuch ads: "Nonsuches do *not* like the accidental jibe."

After that thunderous wake-up call, we were all pretty sprite and perky then, our hearts still thumping and each of us kind of patting down our bodies, checking our limbs. All of us were a little leery about moving the sail back over to starboard to get back on our heading. But, with both Mitch and I easing sheets on each side, we got her moved smoothly back over and finally settled in for a nice downwind run.

It also felt incredibly good to finally kill the stinkpot. She needed a break, too, having chugged us along non-stop overnight for thirteen hours since we had killed her the evening before to check the transmission fluid. Phillip and I were eager to let her cool so we could check the level again to make sure she wasn't bleeding out.

While Mitch's Westerbeke really isn't that loud, it was nice to have that industrial rumble gone. Phillip and I always claim it's our "favorite sound on the boat" when we're about to kill the engine. The wind in the sails and the water dancing by the hull always sounds its crispest the

moment the engine's monotonous chugging ceases.

This was it! We were finally sailing and the Nonsuch was romping! Careful this time to keep a close eye out for any threat of another accidental jibe, we eased the canvas even further out to starboard and watched the boat pick up more speed. As I leaned out over the coaming to watch the water dance by, I heard a distinct rope-sounding rub behind me. I looked up to see the main sheet rubbing on the back of the bimini. The sail on the Nonsuch is so big the main sheets actually run *behind* the bimini and they were now rubbing hard on the corner of the bimini frame. Worried about chafe (which I'll grant myself is a legitimate concern), I wrapped a towel around the sheet at the chafe point and duct-taped it around. We'll call it an "Annie wad" and forego the "patent pending" comment for now. *Why?* Because it shouldn't be patented. It's too dumb of an idea. We'll get back to that.

Not long after we had all settled into the cockpit, the sky to the east started to bloom into a bright pink. We knew the sun was about to rise. Sleepy or not, there is no reason to ever miss that. It marks the start of a new day, a new canvas for adventure and—in our case—another safe night passage behind us. With each passing day, we were getting that boat closer and closer to Pensacola. I figured I could catch up on my sleep when I got home. This was a moment not to be missed.

None of the crew said much as we watched this glowing pink ball start to peek over the horizon. It seems slow when you're staring right at it but if you look away—just for a minute—to another point on the horizon, or some spot on the boat, or your own body, whatever, when you look back, you notice it has changed. The vast expanse that was

once a brilliant yellow-pink is now fading to purple and then blue. It's happening right before you and always quicker than you want it to but you can never stop it. It feels good, though, to know you're savoring it. Time. She just passes more slowly out there.

My Lorde-inspired "not done sailing" shift the night before and that Mitch-silencing sunrise the next morning were probably some of the most memorable moments on the trip for me. They're just sights and feelings I have no way of replicating so I just have to remember them. The photos are great but they're not the same. They can't surround me in crisp salt air, flitter a stray strand of hair on my neck and bring back to me the scent of the sea.

I think we all felt we had kind of made it over a hurdle that night, probably because we had. That offshore passage was definitely the longest of the trip and the furthest offshore, not to mention the same passage that had cost Phillip and I a dinghy, an outboard and some busted davits the last time. It was good to get *those* particular nautical miles behind us and wake to a new day with (most) all of the equipment working and all signs pointing to the Florida panhandle. Getting the Nonsuch across the big bend of Florida was certainly an accomplishment and now—just five or so hours out of the East Pass—we were getting close to achieving it.

But how many times have I said this? Don't get cocky my friends. Just when you start to sigh and let your guard down, Mother Nature likes to scooch across the floor in socks and zap you. *Pow.* Then she laughs about it and runs away like your bratty little sister. Just as we started to settle in for coffee and a nice morning sail, the winds started to kick up, some gnarly clouds started to bubble up to the east, then we saw it. A white crack of lightning across the sky.

"We need to crank soon," Phillip said. With the way the weather was building we knew we were going to have to drop the sail. *Yes, the big huge one that we had not thirty minutes ago raised. Sailing is such fun.* The engine was too hot to touch but with some creative use of a potholder and paper towels, I was able to get the transmission fluid dip stick off in order to get a peek. She still had a nice pink coat on the bottom of the stick, so we were fine there. The oil was a little low but not dangerously so. Phillip decided to forego topping it off this time so we could get the sail down quickly in case the storm jumped on top of us.

We were ready to crank. Phillip tried once, twice, three times a lady, but no dice, which was baffling because she had been running solid for hours, days even, on end. Mitch—still trying to strike a truce with the boat—was staring at the engine panel as if he could will it to work. *"Please start,"* his furrowed brow said. Phillip was stumped, irritated, frowning at the ignition. He didn't want to try again and have it *not* crank for fear of pulling in too much raw water and overflowing the intake.

"I don't think I can kill it again," he said and I thought *"Crank? You mean you don't think you can* crank *it again?"* But, it must have been a fortuitous Freudian slip because just as the words tumbled out of his mouth, Phillip's face lit up in a bit of an "Aha!" realization and he lifted the lazarette lid to check the kill switch. We had done this before many times on our boat—accidentally left the kill switch in the "up" position, so it allows the engine to turn over but prevents it from cranking. It's not a hard thing to do. Like forgetting to put the car in park before turning the engine off. Mitch's boat was still somewhat new to us and the accidental jibe had left us all a little flustered. That definitely did the trick, though. Once the kill switch was down, the engine roared to life and I jumped topside to get the sail down. *Yes, the big one.*

The winds were blowing a good fifteen to eighteen knots by then and it was definitely pushing us around as we turned into the wind to drop the sail, which pointed us right toward the storm. I could see the boys back at the cockpit trying to sheet the sail to center. It was clear they were having trouble. Right when I saw it, I knew. My ill-designed "Annie wad" had put us in a pickle.

"The chafe guard!" I hollered back as I made my way to the cockpit.

Lesson learned. Yes, another. They're all free today in the Nonsuch saga. Do not put the chafe guard on the *line*—which needs to move—if possible, put it on the immovable fixture, which does not. I should have put something on the bimini corner if I was worried about it because where was my chafe guard now? Jammed in the pulley near the stern. I tried scooching it up the line enough to allow us to sheet in and get the sail centered but she wasn't moving fast enough. As I mentioned, we'd had the sail *waaay* out to starboard so there was a lot of line to pull in and a lot of tension on it with the heavy winds. Taped-round terrycloth does not scooch quickly along sheet.

"Get me a knife!" I shouted to Mitch and he grabbed the utility knife we kept near the companionway, for this very purpose I suppose. I started sawing away on the duct tape and—for a brief moment—felt a bit like I had been transported back in time. Back to that fateful night when the three of us were hacking the drowning dinghy off the back of mine and Phillip's Niagara. Phillip had been at the helm then, too, and Mitch had handed me a knife and watched as I sawed through lines. I was struck by a strange reminiscent feeling and thought maybe I needed a new sailing nickname—The Hacker or something like that.

After a few final grunts and shears, I finally made it through the layers of terrycloth and freed the line. It had been my fault for putting the chafe guard on the line, so I deserved to deal with the aftermath. Many lessons to be learned in sailing. Clearly this particularly Annie invention should not be patented anywhere.

With the sail now centered and another hack job completed, we were finally able to drop the sail. Putting the sail cover on, however, in those conditions was an interesting chore. You really had to hold on to something—a handle, a stanchion post, a sheet (although that's not the best thing to grab because it will yank free if not cleated)—but something to keep yourself on the boat while Mitch and I were rocking and rolling and getting blown around up there.

"Move!" Mitch said as I was trying to tiptoe on the stern rail to tie a sail tie around the back end of the sail on top of the bimini. I frowned at first, hating when he issued such terse commands to me, but then I just handed the tie to him and got the heck out of the way. While it is possible for me to reach the sail in the middle of the bimini, it is a bit dangerous doing it while standing on the stern rail in knock-about conditions. Maybe just as much as Mitch reaching over while standing on the coaming (I have some awesome tip-toe abilities) but it was his boat. So it was his call. *Oh alriiight.*

When it was all done, the three of us fell into a heap in the cockpit and kept an eye on the storm. I swear every time we seemed to get offshore in that boat, there was a lightning storm on our horizon. Honestly, I cannot recall a passage during that trip when we were not chased by a rumbling storm. Maybe it was the time of year (late June) or just that part of the state, but I can confidently say there wasn't a day that went by that we did not see lightning. Thankfully, though, it seemed this storm was content to just botch our sunrise sail and then back off. It left us little wind, however, that was (of course!) right on the nose, which meant we had to continue motoring. It seemed to be our favorite thing to do in the Nonsuch.

The winds turned more favorable, though, after we made the turn toward the East Pass so we raised the sail back up around 1:00 p.m. to kill the engine (remembering *this time* to push the kill switch back down) so we could check the fluids again. Yes, those pesky things. Sad-but-true: What goes out must be put back in.

If I said the oil was "low, but not *dangerously* low" that morning when we cranked before the so-called storm, it was now—after five-or-so hours running—nearing danger levels. And so began the adventure of adding oil to the Nonsuch.

We had yet to do this and—this may sound crazy—but when Phillip and I first looked at the engine, just before midnight back in Ft. Myers, we were a little unsure of how exactly you would go about it. The oil cap is literally back about two feet from the front of the engine with maybe ten inches between it and the ceiling of the engine room. It would be difficult to get a funnel in there, much less a bottle of oil *above* said funnel to pour in.

At the time Phillip and I began to ponder it, I think we were secretly hoping we wouldn't have to broach that problem on this trip. *Maybe we'll be able to sail a good bit and we won't have to top off the oil. That'll be Mitch's problem when we get back.* That would have been great! Obviously, that's not what happened. I believe, by this point, we had put a good thirty plus hours on the engine, perhaps forty, I lost count—on this trip alone.

Now it was no longer time to just ponder it. We had to somehow accomplish it because she needed oil. We all kind of scratched our heads a bit then I offered up the one thought that always seems to pop in my head when we talk about catching, pouring or saving fluids.

"Maybe use a water bottle?"

The boys seemed to be on board with this, so I began cutting the bottom end off of a water bottle to use as a substitute for oil-quart-plus-

funnel.

"I'll do it," Mitch offered while I was sawing into the Dasani label, and I think Phillip and I both instinctively just acted like we hadn't heard him. I mentioned the tight space, the two feet back, the little overhead room, as well as the big man known as Mitch who had now offered to perform this circus act. He'd been in long-standing negotiations with the boat since we discovered the transmission fluid leak and I believe he truly thought if he was the one offering her the new deal—a half a quart of oil and you get us to Apalachicola—that she might take it.

"I can do it!" Mitch huffed, sensing our skepticism. Phillip and I knew Mitch would need to get used to doing everything on his own at some point, so I handed him the water bottle/oil bin with about a cup of oil in it and set him to it but I can't tell you how many times Phillip and I asked: "You got it, Mitch?" "You sure?" "Can you see the opening?"

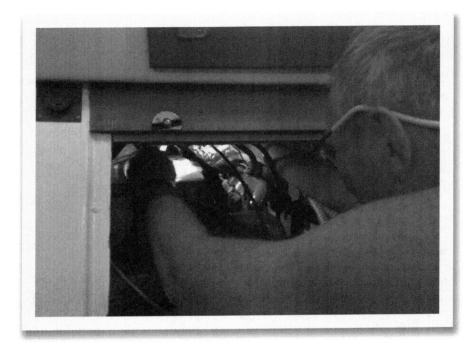

"You sure you got it?"

"Gees guys, would you shut up already? I got this!" Mitch finally said. Phillip and I shared a look and shut up.

Turned out, though, he did. Have it. I was a little surprised, but Mitch displayed some real finesse wiggling into that position and gingerly dumping hacked-off water bottle after bottle of oil in. We checked the fluid level after each dump and determined she looked decent after we had put about a half quart of oil in. Certainly a good bit.

"That'll do ya," I heard Mitch say as he dumped the last bit in. I had to smile at the sight of him literally talking to the Westerbeke. He was still in that bargaining phase, trying to negotiate our way home.

The transmission fluid was also still slowly dripping around the shifter arm so we put a dash more transmission fluid in there too—for safe measure—then deemed her fit to travel. The wind was still steady enough at the time, though, to allow us to keep sailing and, with all of us sweaty, sticky and dirty from the fluid ordeal, Phillip decided it was time for another afternoon dip. *That Mitch and his "just this once" had ruined us!*

While I have never (knock on teak) fallen off of a sailboat when it was under sail, I had also never been allowed to float behind one while it was under sail. The last time we had some "men overboard" during this trip, we were not under sail or motor. We were just bobbing. But, this time, with the boat sailing along at about four knots, it was quite the rush! Phillip tied a throw line behind the boat and we took turns letting the boat drag us along by line or ladder.

Maybe that's not the safest thing to do on an offshore passage, but I really don't care. The conditions were clear, the boat was performing beautifully and was certainly capable of turning around on the unlikely chance one of us accidentally let go.

"Hang on now, Tanglefoot!" Phillip and I hollered to Mitch when it was his time to get in.

It felt incredible—just like a roller coaster ride. I cinched my wrist in the line and let it tug me along, sometimes slowing so my body would ease toward the boat as a wave rolled under her, then pulling me hard and fast with a swift tug as she coasted down the front of a smooth swell. I was all giggles and "Wheees!" the whole time. Fresh cool water whooshed by me and washed every bit of salty sweat off. It was a sailor's dream. I had never done that before and I was so glad Phillip had the

idea.

But again, it was short lived. As soon as we got dried off, we saw big thunderheads rolling up again on the horizon. *Yes, again.* I was actually so irritated by the mere threat of them by now—forcing us each time to raise the sail, drop the sail, raise the sail—that I wanted to curse at the sky: "Shit or get off the pot!" Nearing the inlet to Apalachicola Bay, we were close enough to shore for cell service now and the radar showed a massive pile of yellow and red crap coming toward us. It was time to crank and get that big ass sail down again. Yes, again. *Did I mention it was big?*

"What the heck was that?" Mitch asked right after Phillip cranked. He was leaning over the back stern rail—I had presumed to make sure raw water was coming out as we had taught him (points for you Mitch)— but he also pointed outward, past the stern, at a huge blob of black floating behind us. It was maybe two feet in diameter, with a rainbow-like sheen to it. Obviously oil. We had just cranked and we were the only vessel for miles. Like a turd in the pool, it had obviously come from us. Now we knew where all that oil we had replaced went. I can't say I know exactly what happened or why such a big blob blew out the back of the Nonsuch, but the crew did not take it as a good sign. We made a mental note to pick up some more oil (along with transmission fluid) once we docked in Apalachicola. But, at the time, we needed to keep motoring in order to get the sail down for yet another impending storm.

I could feel it in the air by then. Fifteen minutes prior I had been hot, sweaty and thrilled to death to dip and be dragged in the cool water behind the boat. Now, in my bikini, goose bumps began to form on my arms and my wet hair began chill on my head. The temperature drop was palpable. I'm sure if the barometer on the boat was working, it would have documented a dive.

We all donned our foul weather gear and prepared to drop the sail. Despite my eye-rolling, Mitch insisted we all put on our life jackets as well. *Oh alriiight.* I'm not terrible about wearing mine, I'm just not super eager, particularly in or near protected waters. But, he was the Captain this go-round, so Phillip and I did as we were told. It was probably for the best, too, because that particular sail-drop was the worst we'd endured. Coming into the East Pass, the water was churned up and the Nonsuch was bucking and kicking over two- to three-foot waves, which made the sail flop and misbehave. The wind had picked up too and was batting her and us around.

"Hang on!" Phillip shouted from the cockpit, "but tie her good!" as I made my way topside. "I've got winds over thirty!" he hollered as I grabbed a handrail. It seemed to have come up so suddenly. I was learning that's exactly how summer squalls behave. They are intense, immediate and often short-lived. Mitch and I clung to the flinging sail, grappling with her every two to three feet, practicing our tried and true hug-and-snug method and working each of the sail ties around. The salt from the ties filled my mouth as I clenched them in my teeth and gripped the sail. After Mitch and I got them all tied, we decided to forego the thirty-foot long, fifteen-grommet sail cover for the moment.

Phillip and I were sure after Mitch got the strong track put in on the mast to make raising the sail easier, the very next thing he was likely going to want would be a stack pack to make lowering and covering the sail easier. *If you give a mouse a cookie ...*

And, for whatever reason (I swear I could kill the designer of the Nonsuch for this) but the dodger *used to* grommet down to the coachway roof with stickey-up spikes. That's what I'm going to call them. When there is a dodger there, the spikes stick up through grommets to hold the dodger on the boat and I imagine you would have no real way of stepping on them with a dodger there to stop you. When the dodger is *not* there, however, you have no real way of avoiding them unless you stare entirely at your feet while moving about on deck (not recommended). I planted my bare foot on them approximately 32.4 times during that trip and cursed them every time like it was my first. And you may say deck shoes would have solved that problem. Perhaps. But frankly, I believe they would have pierced right through my rubber soles and held me there, squealing like a stuck pig. I cursed those bloody spikes again several times during this sail-drop ordeal.

With the sail finally contained, though, and the crew thoroughly pooped, we hunkered into the cockpit and watched a wicked lightning storm brew to the north of us in Apalachicola Bay. Lightning seemed to bubble up and percolate, until the cloud would finally boil over and a shocking white streak would jet out. We watched in silence, and probably within just a two-minute time span, as three big bolts broke free and stabbed the ground.

Phillip told Mitch and I to go below and put all of the handheld electronics in the oven, another helpful trick we learned from the infamous delivery skipper, Kretschmer. That way if the boat was struck by lightning, it at least would not zap your phone, laptop, handheld GPS, etc. *He's a smart man that Kretschmer, and that Phillip for remembering such sage advice.* I get great advice all the time. Do I always remember and apply it, however, when said advice would be the most useful? Not usually.

It was strange to think not one hour prior we had been swimming and frolicking on a joyous sailboat amusement ride and now we were geared up in foul weather and life jackets putting the electronics in the oven. It shocked me how quickly our atmosphere could change. But we

felt prepared. The sail was down and lashed. The engine was running strong and we were all tethered in. The three of us sat in the cockpit and watched as the sky to the northeast grew a dark grey and wicked cracks of lightning continued to spear the shore.

I watched as Mitch looked out at the northern sky, his brows pushed up in fret. "Not this time," he whispered out, trying to barter with the burgeoning clouds. I had to wonder what Mitch was promising these higher powers. *If not this time, which?*

CHAPTER SEVEN

DEPRESSION:

The Realization that Foul Weather Will Someday Find You

When the affected finally becomes emotionally connected to the situation, depression will set in. He will isolate himself and become introspective.

CRACK! There went another.

You know, I like to watch lightning. I think it's beautiful. I'm not sure I ever need to see it again from the cockpit of a boat though.

Big thunderheads seemed to loom over us every time we sailed that Nonsuch away from the shore. We had the handheld electronics piled in the oven and Mitch, Phillip and I were all clipped in in the cockpit, watching a gnarly storm brew to the north in Apalachicola Bay. A shelf cloud loomed over the bimini and blotted out the once white, willowy-clouded sky with a massive, impenetrable ledge of grey. All of those times lightning merely loomed in the background and I believe this is the first time the crew thought she was going to finally get us.

Mitch, who usually rattled about with nervous chatter when a storm was looming, now sat, staring straight ahead toward our destination as opposed to the storm. There was no bargaining or trying to negotiate now. It seemed he had accepted the fact that his boat was going to get knocked around in a storm, at some point, on this trip and the realization weighed on him like a lead vest. It was clear he had graduated to stage seven: depression. Soon, his gaze turned away from the horizon to a little bit of fray on the choker line sitting next to him and he just sat and fiddled with it, not talking to anyone.

"Mitch, you okay?" I asked.

"Mmm-hmm," was all I got.

Phillip and I eyed him curiously as he knotted and un-knotted the figure eight on the end of the choker line and kept his eyes down into the cockpit, mesmerized no longer by the white streaks spearing out behind him. Thankfully, at five knots we were moving pretty quickly, *away* from the storm and it seemed the storm wasn't moving much at all. Big bulbous grey clouds sat and dumped on the north shore, leaving us unscathed in the churned-up waters of the bay.

While we were certainly glad the storm skirted us, this time, I believe that marked the moment when Mitch realized they would eventually find his boat someday. No matter how careful you are and how cautious you sail, if you are, in fact, *going* to sail your boat, you are going to get caught in a storm—someday—and the fear and worry that acknowledgement initially brings can be a bit depressing. You work so hard and put so much time and effort into keeping your boat dry, pretty and safe, it's a

tough pill to swallow to know, if you want her and you both to get out and experience adventure, you're probably going to have to watch as another boat punctures her hull, or a shroud breaks loose, or her sail tears, or a hundred other heart-breaking things happen to her. It takes a while for a new boat owner to realize, however, that all of that fear and worry comes with a wealth of joy, accomplishment and pleasure. Mitch hadn't yet seen the crystal green weekends on the water the Nonsuch was going to offer him, the water glistening and cresting off her bow, the dolphins that were going to flip and play alongside her while she sailed. He was still focused now on the likely crashes, bashes and bangs.

Once we tucked into the safety of the Apalachicola River, Mitch's fog seemed to clear. He finally put the choker line down, brought his gaze back up to the horizon and began speaking in more than mere mumbles. *Welcome back buddy!* Talk soon turned to where we would be mooring for the night and Mitch was pushing hard, once again, for AC.

Personally, I was hoping we would stay again at the practically-free City Docks at Apalachicola. There you're greeted with a lone sign hanging on a wayward light pole by the dock that says "Call Chief Bobby Varnes for dockage." The last time Phillip and I had stayed there we got away with a three night stay for thirty dollars total. *I like that Varnes fellow.* But, one thing the City Dock does not afford you is plug-in power and the house batteries on Mitch's boat appeared to be running low. I say "appeared" because the eMeter on the Nonsuch went a little "Jack Sparrow" on us during the trip—speaking coherent battery one moment, rum-infused gibberish the next. Like Jack, she was not to be trusted. So we figured a nice, air-conditioned, rejuvenating night in a slip would be a welcomed reprieve for this tired crew. Also, Mitch has much less draft than we do (4'11") so he can creep further up the Apalachicola river than we can in our Niagara (5'7").

Once again, we made Mitch handle the docking strategy and tell us what lines to tie off in what order as if he were captaining his ship with only the family aboard and he did a pretty good job. Other than one "Slow down buddy!" and a "You mean your *other* starboard?" from Phillip, Mitch slipped her in pretty nicely. It was nice to see the boat tied up and secure with the longest offshore passage of this trip behind her.

It seemed we got the short end of the marina shower straw, though—twice in a row. Back in Clearwater, we'd had hot water but no AC in the shower rooms. What did I call it? A "steam spray?" The minute you stepped out of the water stream you started sweating. Well, this time, in Apalachicola, we had nice, chilly AC in the shower rooms, but no hot water. I'd call this one an Arctic rinse. I had to wonder if perhaps this was tail end of Mitch's bargaining process: *If you're going to withhold the warm shower at least give us AC.* My lips were turning blue and my teeth were chattering by the time I got out of there. I've never been so thankful to step into the humid Florida air and feel beads of sweat start to form on my skin. *Ahh ... nice and muggy again.* Once we were spruced up, it was time to hit the town.

Phillip and I love the old sleepy Florida feel of Apalachicola. It's like it's been frozen back in time. Everyone moves a little slower. They talk a little slower, too, and I kind of like it. I watched as a three-legged cat meandered across Water Street and tucked under a bent-up sheet metal opening in a nautical antiques shop. Old port lights, buoys and markers littered the edge of the sidewalk along the corner of the shop and I was greeted by an upright steel diving suit, complete with round astronaut-style helmet, and a thick-gloved hand posed up in a wave, as we walked in to see what nautical goodies we could find. I imagined, as 1985 models, some of the stuff in there might work pretty well on either of our boats.

"Everything in that bin is five dollars," the cheery, grey-haired woman shouted to us from behind the register pointing at a bulging cardboard box of ropes, pulleys and shackles as we came through the door. The three of us meandered around the quaint little book and trinket shops on Commerce Street for an hour or so before settling on a bit of an indulgent dinner at one of Apalachicola's finest eateries: Up the Creek.

Talk over dinner turned into an insightful and interesting discussion about the accomplishments of the trip thus far—mainly seeing the boat through the hardest and longest leg of the trip. We decided then to take our time the next day motoring "the ditch" up the Apalachicola River, through Lake Wimico and over to Port St. Joe so Mitch could experience it. Phillip and I had often described this passage to Mitch as a jaunt down the ole' Mississip', as if Huck Finn would pull up right next to you on his rickety raft. The Westerbeke had proven herself more than capable of another motor day and departure from Port St. Joe on the other side of the ditch would give us a nice jumping off point to make the last overnight, approximately twenty-four hour run offshore to Pensacola.

After a filling meal, weariness started to set in. It was hard to believe my day had begun some twenty plus hours ago, singing under a smattering of stars. In that time, we had accidentally jibed once, raised and dropped the sail I believed three times (although I couldn't quite count), were chased by approximately three storms (give or take) and had watched as dozens of white strikes of lightning pierced the ground. Oh, *and* we poured approximately thirty-three and a quarter ounces (give or take) of fluids back into the almighty Westerbeke. Those were—for me at least—the most memorable parts of the day but I thought it might be fun to see what Mitch, the new Captain and owner, had taken away from the passage, so I asked him:

"Mitch, what was the best part of the day for you?"

"Docking her," he said pretty quickly, but with a smile, which I could understand. When Phillip and I take our boat on a passage, I do love when we're out sailing, making way, moving our boat from one interesting anchorage to the next, but I had to agree with Mitch. There is a bit of relief and serenity when the boat makes it safely to the next destination and is secure for the night. Tossing the lines to embark on a voyage always comes with a risk, which means there is always a sense of comfort and accomplishment when you make the journey unscathed.

"No, probably that," Mitch qualified it. "And the stars."

I looked up at them as we walked back to the boat that night and, again I had to agree, while they were beautiful, they weren't the same as they had been in Gulf. It was either the sleepy lights of Apalachicola or just the fact that we were on land now, not sailing that boat under a soft black cloak, but there just weren't as many of them it seemed and they weren't quite as bright.

The next morning I found myself facing a kind of peril I have never encountered in all of my cruising: killer bees! Around 6:00 a.m., I stepped out of the boat to stretch my legs and make a little trip to the ladies room (so as not to wake the boys on the boat with the comforting gurgle and chug of the manual head). As I was walking along the sidewalk along the dock behind the Water Street Hotel, about every five or so feet on my path there was a bee sitting on the sidewalk. At first it didn't bother me, there was just one. As I walked by he started to buzz around so I walked a little quicker, but then I encountered another and another and another.

By the time I got to the restrooms I was flailing and swatting and batting them away. I jiggled on the door handle but it was locked and I felt like I already had a swarm on me. *Screw the bathroom!* I decided to run. I was jumping and sprinting and yelping all the way back to the boat and (seriously) hitting a bee with every arm stroke. Those things were on me! The boys got a big laugh about it but I saw them swatting and yelping a little too when they made their own trek to the men's room.

We walked around Apalachicola poking in all of the quirky little shops and B&Bs. The hot Florida sun was up and Mitch was huffing and puffing everywhere—hot as a pregnant cow. He was cracking Phillip and I up flinging every door open with an overly-dramatic sigh and a gulp of the AC. That man is not meant to cross deserts. We found some diesel engine oil at the marina by the City Docks so we stocked up on that as well as transmission fluid to replenish our leaking fluids before motoring the ditch over to Port St. Joe that day. Like clockwork, the storms started brewing on the horizon the minute we started to think about tossing the lines. Egos aside, it was hard *not* to believe they were

chasing us (*and only us!*) on our journey.

We hunkered down in the boat mid-day to let initial squall and its rains pass. While they look pretty intimidating, the summer storms in Florida are usually intense but very brief. They would rumble and flash and dump some rain and then the skies will clear. We spent the stormy hour battened down in the boat replenishing the fluids.

"Why are you putting that on?" Mitch asked as I was tying my bikini around the back.

"It's my work suit," I said, shoulders shrugged because it really was.

Unless I crawl in those grimy spots naked or in just my undies (which I do, often, when it's just Phillip and me), there is nothing else I can wear that offers me less chance of getting oil, grime or gunk on skin (from which it readily washes) as opposed to clothes (from which it does readily not). So, bikini equals work suit.

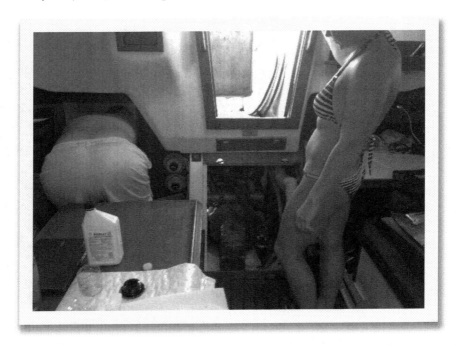

It didn't take long for the storms to pass and the clouds to part. During that time we had put another half-quart of oil in the engine and, while she didn't emit the monstrous "black blob" that had shot out of her the last time we cranked, there was still a little bit of black discharge that floated behind her this time. It was probably a product of us running her harder than she's been run in quite some time, but she really was performing like a champ. Captain Mitch handled the de-docking plan and managed to get all of his "ports" and "starboards" straight this time as we tossed the lines and started puttering up the ditch to Port St. Joe.

The storms stayed on our horizon but never did anything more than sputter and sprinkle on us as we enjoyed a nice, easy day motoring the ditch. The rust on the old, dilapidated turning bridge we motored through spanned eight different shades from red to brown to black and stood on the old waters as a monument to the past, when people traveled more by train than by boat. A few boats passed us by as the Nonsuch moved gracefully along, a beautifully-formed wake trailing behind her. The folks would always wave as they passed or tip their head to you and several complimented Mitch on his "Nice Nonsuch!" In all, it was a nice, relaxing day in comparison to the tumultuous raise-the-sail, drop-the-sail, watch-the-storm day we'd had the day before out in the Gulf. While it may not be quite as "adventurous", there is something to be said about the serenity of traveling in protected waters.

Phillip and I (totally exploiting our role as delivery crew) started talking up Joe Mama's Pizza along the way and the big, lavish Italian dinner we were hoping for once we got to Port St. Joe. They have great wine flights there, incredible sauce-less chicken wings, an awesome made-table-side, twenty-three-ingredient salad that's large enough to feed an entire family (or one Annie) as well as decadent thin-crust pizza. Aren't you hungry now? We love Joe Mama's! Mitch really didn't have a choice in the matter. But, I mean we were un-paid crew. Phillip and I had no remorse cashing in a little of our oil-changing, head-scrubbing,

and helm-holding for an extravagant Italian dinner.

We stopped in first at the fuel dock at Port St. Joe to fuel up for the last leg of the trip and it was clear Mitch's docking skills really were improving. He did the whole thing—docking and de-docking at the fuel dock—on his own. Phillip and I could tell he was really getting a feel for his Nonsuch, which is a fun thing to watch. Now, did he bump a piling or two when slipping up next to his dock for the night? Sure, but who hasn't? You have to get a feel for that too, because it's just going to happen.

Once we were docked, our first mission was to make a Piggly Wiggly run to get some provisions for the last passage of the trip, and Mitch was killing us over this Arizona Green Tea. *Oh, he's trying to be healthy*, you might think. You're crazy. He's trying to not go thirsty. Mitch thinks green Gatorade is just as healthy. And perhaps it is. I have no idea what Arizona puts in their so-called "tea," but I do know Mitch does not enjoy a tasty glass of tasteless water.

He had brought two gallons of the sugary Arizona stuff for the trip (that and thirty-nine, give or take, single servings of Gatorade). Mitch had burned through his two green gallons early on and was now in dire need of more. He meandered the Piggly aisles back and forth with no success and finally enlisted one of the fine red shirt-clad Piggly people to help him on his hunt. Patient as he is, when she couldn't find it in thirty seconds, he enlisted yet another. I swear, Mitch had two little red helpers leading his charge through every aisle of the store looking for his beloved tea, yet he came up empty-handed.

"Alright, where's your Gatorade?" he asked the Piggly crew.

As it often does, provisioning lead to hunger and, as soon as the boat was stocked for the last leg of the trip, the crew ventured out for dinner. While it doesn't have the sleepy port town feel of Apalachicola, Port St. Joe does offer beautiful meandering walkways through some of Florida's most beautiful coast lines. The quaint downtown strip has many great local eateries as well as many shops with a full array of paintings, sculptures, hand-made jewelry, music, plays and other offerings from the town's many native artists.

Port St. Joe definitely has a strong "community" feel to it. So much so the folks at the marina office remembered Phillip and I from our previous stay there on our way down to the Keys the year prior. Granted, we were quite memorable blowing up our twelve-meter kite and bringing in a crowd while kite-surfing in St. Joseph Bay. But it did show they were a small-knit group, excited by, and very welcome to, travelers passing through.

After a few adult beverages at the Haugthy Heron, Phillip and I—emboldened either by the drinks or perhaps our newly-anointed status as delivery skippers, a title also brought on by the drinks—broached the subject, once again, of a big, indulgent dinner "Joe Mama" would be proud of. We had been craving those succulent chicken wings, that tangy salad dressing and the cheesy, meaty goodness of a perfectly-cooked thin crust pizza all afternoon. It's amazing how good you can make food taste in your mind when you think about it all day. Mitch had given us a wealth of entertainment and adventure on this trip, sure, but also enough grief of our own to justify it. We didn't even let Mitch vote. It was Joe Mama's or bust.

"Table for three, please."

Our server was a cute and chatty twenty-something year old with a thick make-up line along her chin and a box the shape of Marlboros in the back pocket of her black, stretch server pants. She made some small talk with us while dropping some linens and plates down, moving pretty quickly, obviously trying (as a good server should) to get us drinks, then appetizers, then the main course. In and out. On to the next. Phillip wasn't having it, though. For he and I, this was one of the highlights of the trip. We were going to do it like the Europeans—nice and slow—and he was trying to find a way to convey that to our server.

"We want to enjoy the … AC in here," Phillip explained. "Because ours is out," as he threw Mitch and I a wink.

"Oh, in the truck or the trailer?" our server asked, not missing a beat.

"Neither. The boat!" we all said heartily, laughing at the fact that we obviously fell well below her, and likely any other upstanding Port St. Joe citizen, on the redneck scale of fine-living.

Dinner at Joe Mama's was such a treat. While Phillip and I don't need a lavish, fine-dining experience every night, the occasional splurge is worth it. Especially after a couple of salty, tiring days at sea. We definitely indulged and it was great of Mitch to treat the crew.

I don't recall much about the walk back to the boat, though. I know there were a lot of replays of the red Piggly ladies and the Arizona tea fiasco and lots of questions about whether the AC was running in our mobile marine home, but that's about it. I recall some bumping of elbows and backsides as we all brushed our teeth around the galley sink and lumbered to our respective bunks. I also know the crew slept nice and soundly that night. *Maybe a little too soundly.*

"No more two bottles of wine for you guys!" Mitch croaked when we all woke the next morning. "Phillip snored all night."

Phillip just smiled and rolled over, which made me smile too. It had been a fun night on the town but the Gulf was calling us back. It was time that day to ready the boat and head offshore again to make our last twenty-four hour run from Port St. Joe to Pensacola. We woke to a crisp sunrise and, for the time being, clear skies. The coffee was brewed, the beds were made and the crew of *s/v Tanglefoot* prepared to make way.

While the winds were very light in the marina, Mitch did a good job of de-docking the boat and easing us away from all those treacherous pilings and docks. *Marinas can be a very dangerous place for boats you know!* Phillip and I could both tell Mitch was getting more and more comfortable single-handing the boat the more we made him do it with us aboard merely as make-shift training wheels." There were many times he was virtually cruising along on his own without any help from us, which was a really cool thing to see. Phillip and I could both easily remember our bump and bumble days and it was fun to watch our friend graduate, as well, from that phase.

The boat was bobbing along in slick, pink water with pelicans just grazing the surface as we motored away from the Port St. Joe Marina into St. Joseph's Bay and steered the Nonsuch toward her last offshore passage toward Pensacola.

It seemed the winds had decided, once again however, that it was simply not our lucky day to sail. They were right on the nose, initially, not enough, then too much. What can I say? It was June in Florida. They call it "light and variable." I call it "finicky and high-maintenance." We kept the motor going for momentum, but it was sail up, then sail down (to reef it), then sail back up, then reef again—kind of frustrating, particularly with the *big* Nonsuch sail—but we were still technically sailing across calm waters, so we had little to complain about.

After seven hours of light winds and unfavorable tacking, though,

Phillip finally decided to give it up. *Poor thing.* He'd been wanting to sail for days on this trip and it just wasn't happening. While we never wanted rough seas and heavy weather, some nice sailing would have been, well … *nice.* But, when we saw we still had thirty hours to go to make it to Pensacola, with already seven hours behind us on what was *supposed* to be a twenty-four- to twenty-six-hour trip total, we decided it was time to drop the sail and just crank on again, relying solely on the Westerbeke to help chug the vessel home in hopes that she would someday do some great sailing in Pensacola Bay.

We were still out there in blue waters, enjoying the vast horizon, no shore in sight, and the calm surroundings. Absent the fickle winds, it really was a beautiful day out in the Gulf. It was hard to imagine some other vessel out there in distress on that flat, still day, but shortly after noon we heard the VHF crackle to life with a distress call.

We had been monitoring Channel 16 for any distress calls and this was the first time we'd heard something significant come over. Even when we can't respond or offer help, Phillip and I have always found these calls intriguing and we like to listen in for several reasons: a) for learning purposes (as we learn more about how to respond to an emergency aboard our own vessel) and b) because it's like going to a NASCAR race for the accidents. You don't want anyone to get hurt, but if you see a car smash against the wall, you're going to get out of your seat and give her a look. And you often only hear one side of the conversation—that of the Coast Guard's because their VHF reach is further—which only adds to the intrigue. We have heard such conversations before play out as follows:

USCG: "How many aboard your vessel sir?"

No response.

USCG: "Where did the leak begin?"

No response.

USCG: "Are you able to keep up with the amount of water coming in?"

gulp

Yeah ... *not* really the conversation you want to hear out on the water. What was the first cackled inquiry we heard from the Coast Guard this time?

USCG: "Where did the fire begin?"

No response.

At first we didn't hear anything. We didn't see anything on the horizon. We had no way of knowing how far away this burning vessel might be. Then we saw a big sport fishing boat blaze across our bow a few miles ahead and the radio crackled back to life.

Fishing Boat: "We're approximately 10 miles from the boat in distress."

The Coast Guard swapped him over from Channel 16 to 22—to which we (of course) swapped over as well in order to listen—before responding:

USCG: "Sport vessel, if you are able, please respond to the vessel in distress, assist as needed and report back. We're an hour and a half out."

All three of us perked up and began looking around the horizon. At first, we couldn't see anything then, faintly after a few minutes, the tiniest cloud of grey began to appear on the horizon. It then deepened in color and began to billow toward the sky. It was right there. We could see it. A vessel on fire!

I watched Mitch's jaw drop when he saw it. That far off, the smoke had to be climbing twenty, maybe thirty feet. I was sure he was imagining—perhaps for the first time now that a real-life example was burning away on the horizon—his own boat on fire and his depression began to creep back in. It was impossible not to feel for whoever owned that blazing boat.

I'm not sure I can imagine much worse on a boat than a fire aboard. Thankfully—after ten pretty intense minutes and a serious exchange between the USCG and the fishing vessel about what the fishing vessel could see, what safety equipment they had on board and proper procedure for approaching the vessel in distress—the fishing boat finally arrived to the scene and reported several people adrift behind the vessel in a life raft and others swimming in the water. The captain of the burning vessel finally got on the radio and told the USCG: "I'm the Captain of the vessel. I'll bet you want to speak to me."

Phillip, Mitch and I nodded fervently in our own little cockpit theatre, playing the armchair Coast Guard. *Umm … yeah!*

Thankfully, the Captain reported that all the crew aboard were safely evacuated, including his eleven-year-old son, but the vessel was a total loss. My heart sank for him. *Can you imagine?* Fortunately they were all safe, but what a sad thing to watch your boat burn on the water. I don't even want to think about it. While Mitch, Phillip and I were not thrilled to be motoring across the Gulf, we were certainly counting our blessings knowing our vessel was intact and chugging along safely toward home port. Sometimes a little perspective can change everything. When fire was the very real alternative, motoring wasn't so bad.

Another reason we were motoring was because we were trying to get Mitch's boat back to the dock in Pensacola by 4:00 p.m. the following day so we could avoid bringing his boat back into a new port (to him) and a new inlet and a new dock (to everyone) in the dark. We cruised along into the afternoon, cleaned up in the cockpit around dusk and settled into a nice evening routine.

But, that's where we made our mistake. I swear we needed some *Oops!* Britney song to accompany this trip because we did it again. Just as we eased into the evening, divvied up the night shifts and decided we were going to have a nice, easy night motoring along, that's when Mother Nature decided just the opposite. Once again (we were haunted by thunderheads on this trip!), big ominous clouds began to billow and build to the north of us and it was just after sunset that we saw our first slither of white against the sky. It was lightning. Again.

It mostly stayed at bay but we decided to put the bimini back up just in case it rained during the night and get our foul weather gear ready, lifejackets and tethers ready. This was not going to be the night for us to cruise gently underneath the stars. There would be no music, no belting

out of incorrect Lorde lyrics, no "dancing in the world alone." None of that. Not this night.

This would be the night that the storms finally caught us. All of those evenings we watched as beautiful storm clouds brewed in the distance, enchanting us with sparks of lightning left and right and this was going to be the night she decided to squat right on top of us.

"Annie," Mitch shook me awake, this time not ripping and stripping himself of foul weather gear on his way to the vberth. I glanced at my phone. It was about ten minutes prior to my shift and once Mitch saw I was awake he headed back up to the cockpit to let me do my get-ready routine, which I was grateful for. *I need my five minutes.* Mitch really was falling into step, but once I made it topside, he wasn't eager to sit around and chat about the weather. In fact it was the topic of the weather, in particular, he wanted to avoid. After a brief exchange of our heading, the status of the motor and autopilot, Mitch left me with "It's getting black," as he made his way down below after our brief report.

As my night vision set in and I could finally make out clearly the horizon—what was left of it at least—I could see Mitch was right. We still had hard winds right on the nose so we were still motoring along fine but the clouds to the north continued to build and blot out the horizon. There was no longer sky and sea to starboard, it was just black. Everywhere black. I eased us off a little more to the west in hopes of avoiding it but she seemed to be bent on chasing us. *"I'll get you my pretties,"* I heard the clouds cackling behind me.

When it was time for me to wake Phillip for his shift at 1:30 a.m., it looked like the storm was about to drop on us at any moment. Rain started circling under the bimini and stinging us from the sides as winds whipped through the rigging. I stayed up with Phillip until 2:00 a.m. to see if the conditions would hold or so I would be ready on deck to help him if they did not.

Phillip and I were both hunkered down by the companionway, hiding from the weather. Thankfully, using our long clips, we could tether to helm but still take cover by the companionway. While Mitch's boat does have a huge bimini, a dodger it does not so the only place to really hide from the spitting rain is curled up under the height of the companionway. The autopilot was holding at the time and Phillip and I were keeping a constant look at the horizon. Phillip would step back behind the helm every ten-or-so minutes to check the instruments and readings and then would come back—shivering and shaking off beads of rain—and hunker down again with me. I watched his face every time, as his eyes darted from instrument to instrument—comforted by the lack of change in his expression, which told me everything was running smoothly. But just as I shifted my gaze back to the horizon, I heard him say it.

"The GPS is out."

I blinked back at him through the rain. "The what?" I asked, although I knew exactly what he had said. I had heard the words. I knew what they were and I knew what each one meant, individually. I just couldn't make my mind put them together and tell me exactly what they meant, as a whole. *The. Out. GPS. Is.*

"It's out," Phillip said again. "It can't seem to find our location."

My gears finally started to turn and knock some rust to the floor of my wet, rattled mind. "Is the compass still lit?" I asked, recalling during our passage in the Niagara across the Gulf that the compass light had flickered a time or two and I thought to myself at the time: *What if both the GPS and the compass light went out?* I'm sure worse has happened to many out there, and I guess you could get a head lamp or put a flash light to light the compass, but you don't really ponder these things until your instruments start dropping one by one.

"Yeah, we've got a heading and the autopilot is holding," Phillip said, "but the storm must be so heavy on us, we can't get a satellite signal. The GPS can't pick us up."

I just stared at him and let out a long sigh. What else was I going to do? The best person to be sitting in front of that gismo trying to make it work was Phillip. I didn't have any brilliant ideas other than restart it. Like a goobered-up computer, just re-boot it. But Phillip knew that was my go-to. There wasn't anything I could tell him he hadn't already thought of or tried.

"Well," I said. "I'll keep a good lookout," I told him, knowing the worst part of a lost GPS was the fact that we couldn't see upcoming obstacles on the screen—buoys, markers, towers, and the other dangerous like. We were offshore. We had plenty of depth. It was hard, though, to see anything on the horizon with the clouds and rain on us. I could barely differentiate the water from the sky, but I kept squinting out, keeping my eyes level with where I *thought* the horizon was in case anything could stand out. Phillip's shift played out like this for another thirty minutes until he sent me down to get some rest around 2:30 a.m.

I heard him rustle Mitch a little before 3:00 a.m. I looked at the clock to note the time and figured (or hoped at least) everything was fine and it was just time for Mitch's shift. Then I heard Mitch and Phillip speaking loudly in the cockpit once Mitch had made his way up there—likely so they could hear each other over the rain and likely because Mitch is just a loud guy—but I could tell by the tone of Mitch's voice that he was worked up. When I heard my name, I cracked open the companionway door and stuck my head out to see what was going on.

"Good, get up here," Mitch said as he grabbed one of my elbows and started to pull me into the cockpit without any of my watch gear on yet. I looked around and then back at Phillip to get some reassurance. The storm was still rolling and churning on our starboard side, still spitting rain on us and beating the boat around in heavy winds. It was closer now, but no more intense than when Phillip and I had been watching it some thirty minutes earlier.

"No," Phillip said. I didn't know what they had been arguing about so I just stood still on the companionway stairs for a moment to see what Phillip wanted me to do. Then it dawned on me. This was Mitch's first time, on his boat, in a storm. The clouds had been ominous when Mitch had gone down below around midnight but they hadn't been this threatening. It hadn't been raining and it hadn't been knocking us about. It was Phillip and I, who had watched them build and Phillip and I who had experienced worse so—for Mitch, and particularly for the first time facing something like this on *his* boat—this was understandably a bit frightening.

"If the storm's going to hit, we should all stay up and weather it together," Mitch said. I remained silent. While I didn't mind staying up another shift if it was needed, I wasn't sure it was and Phillip's was the cue I was going to follow. In situations like this, it always is.

"Why are you going to do that, huh?" Phillip said to Mitch sharply. "You're going to keep us all up and exhaust everyone so that no one is fresh and ready to take over the wheel when your shift is over?"

Mitch sat kind of still for a moment, just blinking and looking at Phillip. I knew he was just worried, scared. There was no selfish or lazy intent here. He just feared for the boat and us and didn't know what the best decision was. This trip—and, more specifically, this leg in particular, handling his own boat in a storm—was going to be a pretty big notch in Mitch's sailing belt. I completely understood why he wanted my help. But Phillip was right. If we all stayed up, we would all be exhausted. If the boys could handle it, they should, so that I could sleep and take over fresh the next shift, which might be worse. I just looked at Mitch, pulled my elbow gently away and told them I was just a shout away if they needed anything.

"We'll let you know," Phillip said. "Put the electronics in the oven and shut the companionway back on your way down."

As I did, I watched Mitch watching me. His eyes were kind of pleading like a dog who doesn't want to be left outside. A part of me felt bad for him but a bigger part did not. This was just part of it. It looked to be a very tolerable storm—uncomfortable, mind you—but tolerable. There's nothing you can do but be as prepared as you can and then just be as smart as you can, which includes ensuring your crew is as rested and well-managed as possible. Phillip was taking one for the team by staying up with Mitch during his shift, and that meant he would really need me to be fresh when my time rolled around. Besides, I knew if the storm hit at the end of Mitch's stint, my 4:00 a.m. shift was going to be hell on black water so rest was the best thing I could do for myself. I closed the top to the companionway, put the electronics in the oven and tucked back down on the settee as I heard thunder rumble in the distance. I hadn't heard Phillip mention anything to Mitch about the GPS being out and I was pretty sure he just wouldn't tell him. Mitch didn't need anything else to worry about right then.

"Annie!"

I heard his voice straining through a little crack in the companionway. It was Mitch, which didn't mean I was *not* worried, but had it been Phillip's I probably would have sprung out of bed and busted through those little companionway saloon doors in two steps.

"Yeah," I said as I sat up on the settee.

"It's your shift," Mitch said.

I hate to admit but I'm sure my shoulders kind of fell and I know a little huff found its way out of me. I was just tired. I'd gone to bed around 10:00 p.m., woke around midnight to hold my shift, gone back to bed close to 3:00 a.m. and now it was 4:00 a.m. and I was about to be back on deck till likely sunrise. Now I know, when it comes to hearty tales of boats at sea—leaking all the way across the Atlantic with a crew that has to stay up around the clock for three days pumping water and holding the helm just to get the boat home—that my little "I'm tired" spiel this particular night means nothing, but at the moment it meant a lot to me. It's just honestly how I felt. Like I wished I could have rolled back over and just kept sleeping.

But when I blinked myself awake and really took in my sights and sounds my adrenaline started to wake me up. I could now see Mitch's head was dripping into the companionway. His hair was wet and I could now hear rain outside on the deck. I hear a gust of wind rip through the cockpit and I heard Mitch's feet scramble as he balanced himself over a wave. I then thought about Phillip who had been up there since 1:30 a.m. and I cursed myself for entertaining my little pouty tired spell even for one minute.

I peeked up through the crack Mitch had made in the companionway opening to see Phillip still at the helm, which I'm sure he had held the entire time. The man does not like to give up the wheel in a storm. He was eyeing the storm still to the north of us and guiding the boat through three- to four-foot rollers, not big by any means but with short periods, they were making for an uncomfortable, challenging passage. I pulled myself into my sweaty foul weather gear and made my way topside. Mitch was now mighty keen on the "crew needs rest" idea— now that it was *his* turn to go below. Or so he thought. As he started to ease up to make his way down below, Phillip stopped him.

"Uh-uh buddy. I need rest."

Mitch looked at him with this half-shocked, half-defeated face. He started to mutter something and Phillip said, "Go down and get a drink, freshen up. Then meet Annie back up here and sit with her through her shift." Mitch opened his mouth. Shut it. Looked around and finally slinked down below. I looked to Phillip after Mitch passed by me and he was sporting an it's-got-to-be-done look.

"It's fine, really" he told me once Mitch was out of ear-shot. "It's just spitting rain at us and pushing the boat around a little, but it's not too bad. I think it will pass in a couple of hours. Maybe before the end of your shift, but he needs this. Mitch needs to feel what it's like."

I definitely agreed, nodding at him. Experiences like this are crucial. They help condition you for the next time, when it may be worse.

"Oh, and the good news," he said. "The GPS is back up. You'll be fine," Phillip said as he patted my shoulder and headed on down. I checked all of the instruments, made sure our engine was plugging along at temp, our autopilot was holding steady and everything else was under control. Phillip was right. It was wet and not very comfortable, but if you've endured worse for longer, it really wasn't that bad. The knocking about of Mitch's Nonsuch that night was nothing compared the bashing Phillip and I had done in our boat the year prior trying to make our way one raging night into Charlotte Harbor. Phillip and I had made the mistake of trying to motor bare poles through rough seas because we thought that was safer than having canvas up in heavy winds. While we have since learned a strategically-placed storm sail would have served us far better, it was each of those uncomfortable twelve hours of beating and crashing through churning waters that taught us that and helped better prepare us for this spitting storm in Mitch's Nonsuch.

Without the benefit of that mistake under his belt, I could tell Mitch was thinking what we were in at the time was bad. Really bad. It wouldn't matter what I said. To him it was bad. I watched as Mitch climbed back up into the cockpit and ducked into his little corner by the companionway. He looked out somberly, watching the clouds and the occasional lightening and bundled himself in his jacket, hardly uttering a word the first half hour. He seemed so withdrawn, so overwhelmed with the burden of bringing his boat home in a storm, of watching instruments and systems fail. I tried to tell him things that made this passage seem better than it must have to him.

"You know we're lucky it's June and so warm out. Otherwise we'd be freezing in this rain."

Nothing.

"It looks like the clouds are finally breaking to the north. I don't think we'll be in this much longer."

Crickets.

I really do think that was Mitch's most depressing moment of the trip. Watching him, his shoulders shrugged up near his ears for protection, wincing every time the boat bashed a wave, he reminded me of myself and how very similar I looked curled up next to the companionway on our Niagara the night our boat fought her way across these same dark waters.

"Can you see the markers?" Phillip shouted to me from the helm. And shout he had to. It was during our trip down to the Keys the year prior when Phillip and I found ourselves in ripping winds and five-foot seas, trying to beat our way back to shore and shouting was the only way we could hear one another.

"No, not yet!" I shouted back. They were engulfed in black chop.

To this day, that is still "my worst" of many things: worst night on passage, worst night on our boat, worst night in the Gulf, etc. Phillip and I—well Phillip, primarily, as he held the helm for twelve hours straight—clawed and climbed our boat, bare poles, out of an angry body of water. With every bash of our hull into a brick wall of water, I swear it sounded like the boat was cracking in half. It was hard to believe—to truly convince yourself—she was not with each thunderous crash. I curled myself up under the dodger, next to the companionway and, like Mitch, sat silent and winced with every blow.

There was no nervous chatter from me that evening, no jokes or smiles. It was the first time I truly realized how exposed our boat was out there in bad weather—how vulnerable—and when the realization sank in, a deep depression followed. I was curled up inside myself, praying the boat would make it and that we all would pull through.

It was also that night, however, that taught me how truly strong and valiant our boat is, the Captain too. They both delivered me out of that dark, raging nightmare and the sense of joy that flooded me when we finally made it into Charlotte Harbor, dropped the hook and found the boat the next day, still floating, still intact, and still beautiful, basking under a blanket of sun like nothing had happened, that I understood the fear I could have for the boat, but also the pride. I wouldn't have known she was capable of that had I not experienced it myself. I knew this experience on the Nonsuch would do the same for Mitch, so I just let him ride it out in silence.

For Phillip and I, while it was uncomfortable, this was the exact type of offshore experience—educational but not dangerous—that we were hoping for so we were soaking it up, buckled in front and center on the Nonsuch to learn from the journey. I doubted Phillip was really that tired. Storms seem to flick on his adrenaline switch. He probably sat down below the whole time doing navigation calculations and fiddling with the handheld GPS.

I think he just went below for a bit for Mitch's sake—to make Mitch push himself farther than he thought he could, because Phillip was back up in no time. Forty-five minutes at the most. And while Mitch had sat there—quiet and downtrodden the entire time—he had also been alert, keen, and had kept a watchful eye on the horizon. While he wouldn't respond to my zippity-doo-dah comments about what a bright, cheerful passage we were making, he had pointed out any potential obstacles he thought he saw and answered all of my serious questions about our course and the conditions.

Did he do it in a mopey little mumble? Yes, but my point is Mitch did it. You don't have to chat and be chipper to perform your duties as crew and Mitch had certainly done his job. Phillip relieved him of his post and Mitch gladly climbed down below for some well-deserved rest while Phillip and I sat up in the spitting rain.

For the most part it remained only that, just stinging rain and an uncomfortable sea state. There was about a twenty-minute spell of hard, driving rain that made Phillip and I both a little uneasy. We could barely hear each other shouting through it, confirming no obstacles were visible on either side (although confirmation was a bit shaky with visibility being so poor). And the GPS went out again during this downpour, but it passed pretty soon, the GPS came back shortly after and it seemed that was the tipping point for the storm as she finally started to dissipate and ease off after that.

We woke Mitch around sunrise to hold his shift. While it was still spattering and pushing us around, our conditions had improved at that point and Mitch stepped right in behind the helm looking like a new man. I don't know what was in the man's Gatorade. Must have been Prozac or something because there wasn't a sliver of depression left. He was all nerves and excitement. *"Look what my boat can do!"* his expression said.

Phillip stretched out on the port side of the cockpit and I remained curled and watchful on the starboard side. Mitch was a little jittery at first, sitting behind the helm, but serving really—as we all had that passage—as only "second in charge" behind the autopilot. Once the storm started easing off, though, his nerves seemed to calm and he was handling the boat well. The true champions that evening were truly the engine and the autopilot. The night would have been far more intimidating and exhausting without them.

I was in and out of sleep, sitting with Mitch in the cockpit, until the sun rose. The storm had cleared by then and we were all grateful to once again be able to differentiate between sky and water. *Ahh ... the horizon! There it is!*

And, it was nice to see something recognizable in our sights.

"There's Destin!" Mitch shouted inadvertently when he saw it.

Phillip woke around 7:30 a.m. and decided we should cut the engine to check the fluids. I really wish I thought about that as much as he does. I'm like that goldfish who is always surprised by the castle. If the engine is running steady, I'm all *Fluids? What fluids? Oh yeah, the fluids!* every time Phillip mentions it. There's a reason he's the Captain on our Niagara. *Good idea boss!*

We were actually all surprised to see they were in fine shape that

morning on the Nonsuch. Somehow we hadn't burned near as much oil while motoring the evening before as our last two passages. We chalked it up to knocking the rust off the old Westie and getting the Nonsuch dialed in a bit tighter. This is what she was meant to do—run! And travel! And she seemed to be liking the adventure. As the crew neared the Pensacola Pass, spirits were soaring. Some flying higher than others apparently.

I pulled out my phone to snap some pictures to memorialize the moment and Mitch, without any prompting, curled one arm up in an old-timey circus pose and spread the goofiest grin on his face. You couldn't *not* take a picture.

"Our champion," Phillip said.

But it was a deed worth celebrating. We had done it! Brought another Hinterhoeller safely home across the Gulf of Mexico.

As we made our way across Pensacola Bay to Bayou Chico, it was hard to believe it had really happened. Mitch, While-You're-Down-There, Roberts had actually bought a boat and—with the help of this hapless crew—chugged her way across the Gulf and cruised her right on in to her new home port. We were all smiles and cheers and one "Slow down buddy" as Mitch tucked his Nonsuch in safely at the dock.

But it was right then and there, not moments after we had safely docked, that the boat began to test him. *What better time, right?* Here it

was, stage eight: testing. Mitch had only booked a temporary slip as he planned to have the Nonsuch hauled out as soon as possible to have the bottom job done and the rub rail and that strut joint repaired that the surveyor had noted. We gave him the number of one of our trusted boat repair experts in Pensacola and Mitch started punching buttons into his phone while Phillip and I were securing and organizing the boat.

"Three weeks!" we heard Mitch scoff as he stuffed a few things haphazardly into a duffel. "Well I'm going to need an estimate," he said as he stepped off the boat and started to walk away—as if that was it, he was done—while the boat sat salty, unplugged and very much un-buttoned up.

"Two grand!" he screeched as he walked the dock, duffel slung over his shoulder like a Hollywood A-lister.

"For what?!"

We warned you buddy.

CHAPTER EIGHT

TESTING:

The Assessment of Your Particular Boat-Project Tolerance

As the affected emerges from depression, he will begin testing various methods of re-activating himself by trying new things and reaching out to support groups or friends to communicate his feelings.

"Yes, I went with the strong tracks," Mitch said to Phillip in a huff. We were talking to him about a week after arriving home from the passage and he had already lined up a local rigger to replace his worn-out reefing lines and—like we had suggested—put in a strong track to help ease raising of the main up the mast. Well, I guess I shouldn't even say "the main." There's only one sail on the Nonsuch, so it's 'the main' one. With the way Mitch's big-ass Nonsuch sail squealed and yelped its way to the top of the mast during our passage, he certainly needed something strong to help ease her up there.

"But not the stack pack?" I heard Phillip say. We were really surprised—especially with how much effort it took to unroll that thirty foot scroll known as a sail cover the length of the boat and perform the hug-and-snug maneuver at two-foot intervals all the way down—that Mitch didn't opt for the stack pack. I tuned in, wanting to know his reasoning.

"Well, I ..." I heard Mitch's voice crackle on the other end. "I just. Not now. That sail cover's not too much trouble for now, right?"

It was funny to hear Mitch ask this of Phillip, as if he hadn't been there—right there with me on the bow of that crashing-around boat—wrestling those stupid grommets, while stepping on the old dodger stickey-up spikes. And, what was funny is Mitch and I had wrestled the sail cover together far more than Phillip had. Phillip likes to hold the helm. After mine and Mitch's many arduous stints hoisting, reefing, lowering, re-hoisting and tying down the one-sail on the Nonsuch, I was starting to see why. Fighting that sail cover on and off had been one of the more frustrating chores of the trip. Sometimes we left it off because it was more work than it was worth. But, I guess Mitch found the $2,000 price tag for the stack pack to be more money than *it* was worth. It's funny how you re-value things once they have a price tag on them. Phillip and I were sure Mitch would change his mind in time on that one but perhaps he needed to step on those stupid spikes two thousand times first.

While he did hire out most of the big jobs—the strong track, the bottom job, the rub rail and strut repair—Mitch vowed he was going to do many of the smaller projects himself and that was where Phillip and I liked to call often to check on him and assess his progress.

"How are you doing on that teak varnish, buddy."

"Good, good," Mitch would sigh. "I put one solid coat on the coaming."

"Just one?" Phillip would ask.

"Yeah, why. How many does it need?" Mitch screeched, irritation simmering in his voice.

"Oh, I'd say ten. Eleven at least," Phillip would say, smiling on the other end of the line.

Once the varnish proved to be a little too daunting, Mitch started reaching out to others—online owners forums and other Nonsuch owners—to see what they used.

"I found this Cetol stain that just needs a couple of coats," he told us one day.

"Ahhh … " Phillip said. "That sounds nice. Were you able to lay a few coats down everywhere?"

"Yeah, everywhere, except under the rub rail. I can't bend over like that," he said, as if his impossibility to do it meant it simply couldn't be done. *It's called a dinghy-scaffold. Give it a whirl.* Yet I couldn't quite bring myself to picture Mitch trying to balance himself while standing in his eight-foot Walker Bay while painting upside down. *Okay, forget the underside.*

Mitch really was being a pretty good sport about everything though. He did far more on the boat than I thought he would. Even several things I would have never dreamed of doing, like painting the life ring a new pearly white.

"Looks good, right?" he asked me through a lopsided smile when we went out with him on the boat one day to check out the new strong track and reefing lines.

"Yeah, it does," I had to admit, although I would have never thought to change the color of that thing from the standard yellow you see on so many cruising boats out there to something that "blends" better with the boat. *If I'm wrapping my head around the device correctly—as something you need to be able to see and grab quickly in an emergency—you don't really want it to blend, do you?*

But I couldn't fault Mitch. When you first start doing projects on your boat, you want to do the necessary ones—the safety, performance, critical ones, sure—but once those are completed or scheduled, your mind turns to the fun ones. The cosmetic, comfort things that you have just been dying to do to the boat. I guess, for Mitch, painting the life ring a pretty white was one.

What really cracked Phillip and I up, though, was his suffering through the handrail project. When we were bringing the boat back from Ft. Myers, Phillip had noticed a pretty significant, long-time leak in the spice cabinet above the sink in the galley. It seemed to be coming from one of the screws holding the handrail on the deck. Ironically, Phillip and I had recently removed our handrails on the Niagara and had re-bedded them for the same reason so we had a good understanding of what the project entailed. Mitch did not.

"I did try to take all the screws out," he told Phillip one day. "But it won't come off!" I have to admit I was getting a monstrous chuckle from this one. We had faced the same stinking problem when Phillip and I had popped ours. Apparently screws that stay in place for thirty plus years tend to deteriorate and lose their screw-in, screw-out abilities.

"Did the entire screw come out of each hole?" Phillip asked.

"Well, some were shorter than others, but ..." Mitch trailed off, seeming to put two and two together on his own. "You mean some are still?" "Well how do I?" *Huff.*

To be fair, the handrail project was a pretty substantial one for us at the time—that was before we took on a pretty significant re-fit on the Niagara over the course of the following winter. It was harder than I would have imagined to get the handrails off. I don't believe they're glued on, but whatever sealant they'd used back in 1985 had since morphed into super Gorilla glue, or whatever might be the next homo sapien in the evolutionary adhesive chain. That's the type of un-stickable glue we were dealing with. Even when we did get them off, more holes than not were left with a broke-off screw shaft wedged deep up inside, preventing us from screwing the rails back on. We had to seek the advice of an expert then dig and smoke them out with roll pins. 'Twas not fun.

Sadly, Mitch faced the same predicament when he tried to pop his handrails off to repair the leak. The last time we checked on the status of Mitch's handrail re-bed project, he gave us a line we've since used for many-a-boat-project (and there have been hundreds) that have given Phillip and I Mitch-worthy headaches:

"Phil, I'll have to admit. I've lost enthusiasm for these handrails."

I find myself crammed up, sweaty and greasy, trying to pretzel myself around the manifold in the engine room and I drop another nut, it's: "Phillip, I've lost enthusiasm for these steering cables." Phillip finds himself upside down in a lazarette, shaking muscles, struggling to get a wrench on a bolt and the lazarette lid drops on his shins for the third time, he says: "Annie, I've lost enthusiasm for this chain plate."

But Mitch kept puttering through, cutting checks where he needed to, griping every step of the way, but still stepping up and doing far more than I imagined he would when his hopes of buying his very own boat were just that—hopes. He was passing through this "testing" phase with flying colors. Soon it came time his boat was "ready enough" to get out for the weekend and he feverishly coordinated with us as to when we were planning to leave the dock, how long we thought it would take us to get to the anchorage, how many other boats we thought would be there. All questions we really couldn't answer. Cruising requires a very flexible schedule and a laidback we'll-figure-it-out-when-we-get-there mentality.

But Mitch's excitement was almost cute. We could tell he was just anxious about taking his boat out without us on board and, for the first time, securing her somewhere that wasn't next to a dock. I knew he was going to ask it before he even did, and I knew—even though he was impressing us and improving daily as a tried and true boat owner—what my answer would immediately be:

"We're going to raft up, right?" Mitch asked.

CHAPTER NINE

ACCEPTANCE:

A Final Understanding of the Frustration and Fulfillment Boats Bring

Gradually, the affected will begin to accept the reality of the situation. As he recovers his outlook on life will improve and become more positive. He will still feel the impact but be able to experience it more objectively and less emotionally.

"Slow down, buddy!" Phillip hollered across the water to him. "Slower than that."

I don't know why that man feels he needs to drive his boat that fast. I think it's like nervous laughter. It's because he's a little nervous that he presses hard on the gas. *Throttle that girl down,* I was thinking. *Hell, throw her in reverse!*

Thankfully Phillip knew my stance on the raft-up with Mitch and while he did not share it as strongly, Phillip agreed it would likely be a safer bet to let Mitch anchor at first and save the tedious maneuvering of a raft-up for a future date when he was a little more comfortable with the boat. Besides, he needed to learn how to drop the hook and secure the boat on his own anyway. So, here he came, barreling in to one of our favorite local anchorages in Pensacola, Ft. McRee, where Phillip and I were anchored on our Niagara along with five or six other boats in the anchorage.

This was going to be Mitch's first time anchoring the Nonsuch overnight so he was understandably anxious. It takes a few mooring mishaps to get a feel for how much anchor rode to let out, what type of anchor holds best in what kind of bottom, and what your swing radius is. Well, I should say your "actual" swing radius, which you will learn—the first time you bump a marker, dock or neighboring boat—is bigger than your estimated swing radius.

Mitch was watching Phillip intently, waiting for his cue as to when he should put her in neutral and run forward to drop the hook. I could tell he wanted to ask every five seconds: "Okay now?" "Now?" NOW?!" But he didn't. He just kept easing and waiting and Phillip kept watching until finally:

"Okay now!" Phillip hollered. When he did, Mitch slowed the boat down, skipped up to the bow, wrestled around and cursed a bit, then we heard his chain start to rattle out. Because he had been going so fast he had cruised a bit past the mark we would have liked for him to have dropped at by the time he finally freed the anchor, but he was still in good shape.

Mitch started watching Phillip again, with that same expression *"Tell me when?"* as his twenty feet of chain dropped out and rope followed. Phillip took a long pull from his drink, watching slowly, knowing it wasn't time to drop yet but (I knew!) secretly enjoying his role as Mitch's cruising mentor. Mitch couldn't help himself. He's like a dog that pisses when he's excited.

"More!?" he squealed across the water.

"More!" Phillip answered firmly.

After it appeared fifty or sixty feet had dropped out, Phillip finally called out to him, "Okay, that's good."

"Good? Good!" Mitch hollered back, more out of enthusiasm than an attempt to communicate.

Phillip and I were kicked back in our deck chairs topside, watching Mitch as he cleated the anchor off using a snubber like we had shown him. We watched as he huffed and puffed that stupid long sail cover up onto the deck and huffed and puffed it down the length of the stupid long sail. Our eyes stayed on him as he hugged-and-snugged every grommet in place and got the sail covered and secured nicely. We listened as the pulleys on his davits squeaked out while he lowered his little Walker Bay into the water and we watched as he lowered his 2.5 hp outboard by hand to the dinghy and let it land with a thud in the bottom.

I threw Phillip an *"Is that okay?"* look and he waved off my concern, pushing his lower lip out and nodding his head. Mitch continued to entertain us as he grunted and sloshed and wrestled the outboard onto the transom then tugged and cursed and yanked the little motor to life. He whizzed around in sloppy S-curves, getting a feel for the range of the tiller, as he motored over toward us. Then I watched in pure surprise as he slowly ambled up to our boat, the only contact being his hands on the toe rail as he held off his little boat. There was no "Hang on!" "Hold it" or "Move!" and there was no gut-wrenching crunching of fiberglass.

Phillip and I both looked down at our friend in admiration. He had spawned two huge lakes of sweat underneath both arms as well as deep wet V around his neck. His hands were all nicked up from the boat projects he had been doing the past few weeks and his neck was a bright shade of reddish-brown. I swear he even looked like he'd lost five or ten pounds. Mitch was exhausted, sore and broke but he was smiling. Sweat

and grease covered his brow but he was smiling! Mitch now knew the time, money and work the boat required, but he also knew the reward. I recognized it the minute I saw his face. Acceptance.

"Believe me my young friend there is nothing—absolutely nothing—half so much worth doing as simply messing about in boats. In or out of 'em, it doesn't matter. Nothing seems really to matter, that's the charm of it. Whether you get away, or whether you don't; whether you arrive at your destination or whether you reach somewhere else, or whether you never get anywhere at all, you're always busy, and you never do anything in particular; and when you've done it, there's always something else to do."

— Kenneth Grahame, author of *Wind in the Willows*

About the Author

In a former life, Annie Dike was a trial attorney. Six years in the practice taught her two very important things: 1) she loves to write, but 2) she hates to do it in a fluorescent-lit office. At twenty-nine, Annie stepped away with the clear mindset to travel, to sail, to live a different day every day and write about all of it. Annie now writes and films full-time and spends the majority of her days with the Captain cruising their 35-foot Niagara sailboat around Florida's west coast. Her debut non-fiction pieces, *Salt of a Sailor* and *Keys to the Kingdom*, were Amazon #1 bestsellers in sailing books. Check out Annie's other books on Amazon and follow her many (mis)adventures via her blogs, photos and YouTube videos at www.HaveWindWillTravel.com.

Made in the USA
Middletown, DE
25 May 2016